What's So Funny About Education?

Lou Fournier

What's So Funny About Education?

Foreword by
David D. Thornburg

Illustrated by Tom McKeith

CORWIN PRESS, INC.
A Sage Publications Company
Thousand Oaks, California

For information:

Corwin Press, Inc.
A Sage Publications Company
2455 Teller Road
Thousand Oaks, California 91320
www.corwinpress.com

Sage Publications Ltd.
6 Bonhill Street
London EC2A 4PU
United Kingdom

Sage Publications India Pvt. Ltd.
B-42, Panchsheel Enclave
Post Box 4109
New Delhi 110 017 India

Library of Congress Cataloging-in-Publication Data

Fournier, Lou.
What's so funny about education? /
by Lou Fournier ; illustrations by Tom McKeith.
    p. cm.
ISBN 0-7619-3933-4 (Cloth) — ISBN 0-7619-3934-2 (Paper)
    1. Schools—Humor. 2. Education—Humor. I. Title.
PN6231.S3F68 2003
818´.602—dc21

                                        2003007607

03 04 05 06 10 9 8 7 6 5 4 3 2 1

Acquisitions editor:	Robb Clouse
Editorial assistant:	Jingle Vea
Production editor:	Sanford Robinson
Proofreader:	Nevair Kabakian
Cover designer:	Tracy Miller
Production artist:	Lisa Miller

Contents

About the Author

Lou Fournier is an Associate in the Thornburg Center for Professional Development. He is coauthor of *Enlighten Up! An Educator's Guide to Stress-Free Living* (ASCD 2003) and author of *Power and Purpose* (2003). He has had careers in journalism, training and development, music, marketing, and as a corporate executive for education technology companies. Lou has been a guest of the president at the White House. His insights into purposeful use of music have been filmed for a a Master's degree program for Walden University by Canter & Associates. He wrote a monthly humor column for *Converge* magazine. In the field of music, Lou has won numerous awards for songwriting and performing.

About the Illustrator

Tom McKeith was born in Dumbarton, Scotland, in 1948. He moved to the USA at the age of 22 to study photography at the University of Connecticut. Subsequently he moved to California to continue his studies. He had the great fortune of spending five summers studying with Ansel Adams at his Photographic Workshops in Carmel. Having attained a Master's Degree in Photography at California State University at Fullerton, he began teaching the subject at California State University at Los Angeles. At the same time he was also carving a niche for himself as an illustrator in the magazine and book publishing industry. It was this circumstance which led him to move to Sacramento, California, where he was offered a position as an editorial illustrator for e.Republic.

Acknowledgments

Corwin Press gratefully acknowledges the contributions of the following reviewers:

Michelle Lampher
Director, Marketing, Sales, and Publishing
National Association of Secondary Principals
Reston, VA

Sara Armstrong, Ph.D.
Director of Content
The George Lucas Educational Foundation
San Rafael, CA

George E. Pawlas
Professor
Educational Research, Technology, & Leadership
University of Central Florida
Orlando, FL

David Thornburg
Author and Consultant
Lake Barrington, IL

Mary Kay Morrison
Education Consultant
Kishwaukee Intermediate Delivery System (KIDS)
Illinois Regional Offices of Education
Loves Park, IL

Foreword

There have been few times in history when we have needed humor more than we do today. And nowhere is this more true than in the field of education. As education is pulled this way and that, the humorist's role helps maintain perspective on a life that seems to be spinning out of control. Educators who have lived through a career filled with educational reforms du jour (French for "with sauce") are now expected to be technology experts as well as masters of their subject areas. Many long for the old days when a hard drive was a forty-minute commute, not a place to lose word processor files. And, in these times of rapid change, young people are gaining mastery of the Internet and exploring topics that reach far beyond the scope of the teacher's task for the year. Who among us has not marveled at the ability of an art history student to create a fifty-thousand word monograph on the origins of black velvet art? The mind boggles.

When I was asked to write a few words to introduce this volume, I was flattered. Yes, it is true that I am a well-known public speaker, author, and (with Lou) a bluesman of ill-repute—in fact it has been said that my talent runs the gamut from A to C.

But enough about me.

The volume you hold in your hand contains nuggets—pellets, even—of wisdom scattered throughout, all presented with tongue planted firmly in cheek. Now for Lou to have written eloquent humor on the topic of education is a much harder task than, for example, writing something funny about Chicago politics. But he has forged ahead in his quest to bring at least a smile, if not outright guffaws to his audience. After all, what is so funny about education? Is it funny that your great-grandparents could walk into a classroom today and recognize exactly where they were? Is it funny that we design schools without actively engaging student opinion on how they should be set up? Is it funny that the political leaders who call for more stringent testing are unwilling to take the very tests they propose for our youth? Is it funny that a large state adopted a new science textbook that misidentified the phases of the moon?

Well yes, actually, it is hysterical.

A wise man once said, "If you can keep your head while those around you are losing theirs, perhaps you don't understand the situation." The situation in education today is one in which we need, if not to lose our heads, to shake them joyously in laughter.

Your author, Lou Fournier, has accepted the challenge to cast education's foibles onto a well-lit stage where we can chuckle (and chortle, if so inclined) while acknowledging the underlying truth—a truth we can then choose to address in more serious terms once we have put it in perspective.

Lou has firmly placed one foot in the pragmatic world of today, while with the other he salutes a future view of education where teachers and students are treated with respect, and all learners achieve to the best of their abilities. He does this through the medium of humor, and you are in for a genuine treat.

Enjoy.

David D. Thornburg, Ph.D.
Director, Thornburg Center
Lake Barrington, Illinois

Dog Days of Leadership

I was contemplating the need for leadership in my school just the other day, when I chanced to observe my fierce, take-no-prisoners Doberman, Fluffy, as he chased a car down the road. I felt an obscure yet possibly significant parallel between leadership and dogs chasing cars gently rising to the surface of my mind. I decided to speak with Fluffy about his strange habit.

"Fluffy!" I called as he was returning from an assault on a sports car. "Come here and drop that rear axle right now." The axle rang like wind-chimes down the street, and Fluffy playfully approached me.

"Now, Fluffy, it comes to me that your car chasing may hold a clue to valuable qualities in innovative leadership. But to discern it fully, I must ask: Why, Fluffy, why? Why do you chase cars? Is it a visceral response to some powerful, ancient drive to achieve? Is it a manifestation of your need to excel? Does it reveal your disdain for the ordinary? Is it a call to greatness as only dogs may know it? And do you have the remotest idea what you would do with a car if you caught all of it?"

Fluffy responded in that Zen-like, inscrutable way of his by trying to

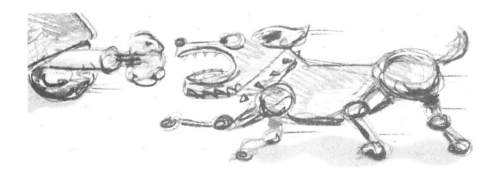

eat my shoes. I got them off my feet in the nick of time and left his presence to further contemplate his sagacity.

I, of course, was a recognized leader in my school. Many of the other teachers and several of my students could greet me by name, if pressed. You don't teach classes like creative thinking and life metaphors in X-Box without gathering a little acclaim. So I was the natural choice to conduct a scholarly research of leadership qualities with a view towards bringing in some new top talent to our institution.

I decided to establish a leadership institute at the school. I would make it open to everyone who demonstrated the ideal qualities of leadership in education for the 21st century. I placed ads for leaders in the newspaper and monitored the responses, from initial letters right through the final interviewing process.

Within days of placing the ads, I had hundreds of responses. I began with a thorough screening process of the letters. I tossed any that began with the salutations "Yo," "Dude," and "Dear Sentient Being." I narrowed my candidates down to a handful and arranged interviews. Some were most telling.

"So tell me," I asked one candidate, "if we choose you, how long would you stay with us?"

"I don't know," he answered. "How late are you open?"

"You do understand, this is a school, a place of learning, not a business. As a leader, you would be expected to be here as long as required to ensure the proper functioning of the institution."

"Hey, no problem. That was my policy at my last institution, until I was released for good behavior."

"Can you give me both a financial and a personal reference?"

"Sure. My bookie and my parole officer."

"Would you describe a time when your work was criticized?"

"No."

"Can you tell me about any special awards you've received?"

"I have been informed that I may already be a winner in several national sweepstakes."

"What features of your previous job have you disliked?"

"Having to produce results, the requirement to put in a certain amount of time and responsibility."

"What are your short-range goals?"

"I dunno. Grab a bite to eat, catch a movie."

"Why do you feel you have top management potential?"

"I don't think 'Dilbert' is funny."

After exhaustive and lengthy interviews, I chose several candidates for my new leadership institute. They included a woman who wrote a compelling essay on the exigencies of new leadership; a gentleman who swore that he, once a professional wrestler, had become state superintendent of education in his state; and Fluffy, who, frankly, interviewed best.

We had our first institute planning session soon thereafter. Our immediate agenda was adoption of a leadership mission statement, one that I insisted must ignite the imagination and serve as a call to action for leaders everywhere.

"I think we must begin with defining a good school leader," the woman said. "This must be someone well-versed in people skills yet fully fluent in the technologies that are changing the world. Someone unafraid to take risks that could bring the best changes. Someone ready to push back the boundaries of seclusion and ordinariness."

"Excellent," I agreed.

"Yet we must also reach out to those around us," the former pro wrestler added.

"So we can include them in the all-important issues facing education?" I asked.

"Well, yeah, that too, I suppose. I was thinking more so we can tag our teammates, and they can jump into the ring and throw those pesky education issues to the mat like they were Gorgo the Hideous."

"I see."

"Woof," added Fluffy, while chewing on a brake pad.

"Well put," I concurred. "Let's discuss direction next. Where do we feel leadership must go in the coming century?"

"Clearly it must address the growing concerns of an increasingly diverse population," the woman said, "ensuring the rights of all to a comprehensive and rewarding education."

"Absolutely," I said.

"And it must look to new boundaries," the wrestler added.

"So as to embrace the stark new realities of the future?" I inquired.

"Well, yeah, that too. I was thinking more of seating in classrooms. You know how in the ring the people up in those cheap seats can barely see you when you drop-kick an opponent? We can't have kids in the back seats of our classrooms missing out on all that hot action up front."

"I'd never looked at it from that point of view," I confessed.

"Arf," commented Fluffy, who then abruptly leapt through the window after a passing car. The window was not open at the time, so the noise really startled us. As I watched Fluffy charge an elderly Saab, it suddenly became clear to me how it was that dogs chasing cars is like leadership. The realization of the moment crystallized soon after, as Fluffy dragged the Saab back to the schoolyard and shook it like a rag doll, depositing the driver, surprised but unhurt, on the ground.

"Fluffy!" I cried in amazement and admiration. "You finally caught a car!"

Fluffy seemed confused at this accomplishment. His greatest triumph was at hand, yet now he could only distract himself by trying to lick the Saab's hubcaps until they shined with slobber. I could see the existential crisis in his eyes as he then chased the driver up the school flagpole.

A leader's quest, Fluffy was telling me, can never be reached. It is the pursuit of the impossible, the reaching of one goal only to be faced with the challenge of a new one.
Atta boy, Fluffy.

Get the Third Degree
From EIT

"Degrees! Degrees! Getchyer red-hot degrees!" How many times have you heard that cry from the degree vendor at the mall, ballpark, or street corner? If you're like most people, probably never. Well, here at the Elvis Institute of Technology (EIT) we're prouder than pigs in fresh slop to tell you that, finally, you can get your own advanced time-share degree!

Hi, I'm Dr. Elvis, Ph.D., L.C.D., R.S.V.P. Right now you're asking yourself, "But Dr. Elvis, what exactly is an advanced time-share degree?" Now, the advanced time-share degree is a concept that we've licensed from its originator, Dr. David Thornburg. One day he was approached to do a project on polysyllabic pseudoerudition, and he said to himself, "If only I also had a Ph.D. in that area!" Then the idea hit him: Why not issue Ph.D.s that can be quickly obtained, very affordable and time-shared, like condos? He floated the idea around the academic community where it got a boisterous reception; nonetheless he continued to refine the concept.

We'd met a few times socially and he knew my renown for bold entrepreneurial enterprises—my first major success was starting the First Church of the Astral Pastor as a combination church and laundromat. I was thunderstruck by his plan and the details he added to it, many of which are recounted in this piece. Our first planning meetings were small, rowdy gatherings down at our local pub, The Jolly Doofus. Within days, we'd launched the Elvis Institute of Technology, and within weeks we were issuing Ph.D.s in a plethora of subject areas, with recipients able to enjoy successes beyond their most reckless reckonings. Now a person with a Ph.D. in one field who needed a degree in another just for a short project, could find an EIT graduate with exactly that degree and use it just for that time, while the other graduate could time-share the first person's degree at the same time. And all EIT degrees are absolutely free! I know what you're thinking: How come no one thought of this before? Some ideas are simply destined to await their proper time, I suppose.

You can also add lots of new letters after your name with EIT, since we offer degrees in areas too adventurous for more timid institutions. Take the letters after my name. "L.C.D." is "Licensed Competent Dude," which, you'll have to admit, sounds pretty impressive and covers a lot of ground. "R.S.V.P." is "Righteous Super Visionary Person," and I can't begin to tell you how many free dinners that's gotten me.

And only EIT offers degrees in both Celsius and Fahrenheit. Our forward-thinking curricula include our patented 360 Degrees (a degree for each day of the year, minus religious holidays), the Turn-Yourself-Around package (180 degrees, sung to the tune of the "Hokey Pokey"), and our acclaimed Third Degree, one so esoteric I cannot describe it without inducing a state of profound awe and/or slumber.

Now, say you want a degree in letters. Most educational institutions won't even let you choose which letters you want. Not EIT. Here you can choose consonants or vowels or, for a special package price, a combination of both. Punctuation, understandably, is extra. For an additional modest fee, we'll even run a spell check.

Ever since Dr. Thornburg announced the initiation of the EIT time-share degree program earlier this year, the response has been overwhelming. Just yesterday a letter poured in. The phone has rarely left the hook. Clearly this is a program destined to impact tens of people.

Testimonials about the EIT program have been coerced from several prominent educators. Take this one, from a magazine editor, who said of EIT, "It's cool! After receiving my R.E.M. degree [Respected Editorial Mogul], my rise to the top was nothing less than coincidental!" A notorious professorial nerdette wrote in, saying, "The EIT degree I acquired just last week has already brought me more junk mail than I ever dreamed possible." Yesterday, I asked a checkout clerk at my local computer super-store what he thought of his EIT degree. "I keep it taped to my register," he said. "It's a real babe magnet."

You may wonder how EIT makes money, since our degrees are free. One of our revenue models involves our deep regard for personal securi-ty issues. We want to make it very easy to protect your identity once you acquire a degree from us. Our Universal Confidentiality Agreement gives you the peace of mind of knowing that no one will ever hear of your asso-ciation with EIT, and it comes with a very affordable monthly payment plan.

Let's face it, in education, real leaders with real innovation are made, not born. That's why the EIT Fast-Track Leadership Authority Program (F.L.A.P.) was created. F.L.A.P. leaders stand out in their fields, like cows. Why surf the Net when you can graze it? Remember that it's a tough, competitive world out there, with as many as three applicants for every 10 open administrative positions. You'll be glad you had the extra edge from the letters F.L.A.P. after your name.

Technologically, EIT is cutting edge. All our courses are entirely online; students never have to come to our offices, which you'll find especially helpful since we tend to change our address a lot. We're planning to hook up with state lottery outlets, so that we'll always have access to a broad-band connection, even if the school right next door can't get one.

We at EIT know that you made it all the way through undergrad school without having to read, and we're darned if we're going to place unreasonable demands on you now. We give you a break. You don't have to read one book to get your EIT degree. You just have to buy the books through our online bookstore. We start you off with a comfortable mini-mum of $100 worth of titles. Graduation automatically gets you a mem-bership in the EIT Book Club, which conveniently sends you a new title every month, whether you return those cards declining the selections or not. You can review new books free for 30 days before being automatical-ly charged for them. Recent hit selections include "I Was a Teenage Techie," "The Name's Bond—School Bond," and the chart-topping "Aligning Your Students' Bodily Functions to State Standards."

We're proud of EIT and its many profit centers. Our school motto, "Learnum est facil," pretty much says it all. We've come a long way since our first degrees. The respect EIT graduates have earned is the envy of none! Come, get degreed with EIT!

Quantum Connections and the Flea Market School
Rummaging for a Hallmark of Great Leadership

I was out in the great Midwest, just north of the lesser one, over the Easter holiday this year. After a delightful dinner, the conversation turned, as after-dinner conversations are wont to do, to the topic of Elvis and ferrets.

This is actually true.

My new friends Ed and Leslie started it. (How can you not instantly befriend people who partake in a conversation about Elvis and ferrets?) Well, strictly speaking, I kicked things off with Elvis by talking about the fact that the renowned Elvis Institute of Technology had recently added some exciting new professional development programs to its Time-Share Ph.D. program. But they got on ferrets. Really. I'm darned if I remember how. But at one point, the conversation went something like this:

"So, Lou, what exactly do you know about Elvis and ferrets?" Ed inquired.

"I can't say I know much about the two together," I remarked.

"That's OK," Ed said understandingly. "Start with anything you know about either one."

"Well, ferrets are little animals that look like thick spaghetti with fur and eyes."

"That's good," said Leslie. "Do you mind if I use that?"

"Where?"

Leslie, as it turns out, heads the library at a mighty and respected university, and she's always getting asked questions like, "What's a ferret?" And that's the connection between Elvis/ferrets and education, as you were doubtless wondering.

It may seem that I digress from my main topic. I can do that. I'm anointed by my publisher to write funny. As we will shortly see, however, this very act of digression is itself quite germane to my point of discussion today. I'll get back to that in a moment, if I feel like it. But now, watch closely as I transition with astonishing literary grace from Elvitic ferrets to my main topic.

Did you know that Elvis once thought seriously of adding ferrets to his act? The union wouldn't let him; otherwise he would've forged a bold new path, musical leader and innovator that he was, into entertainment history. And speaking of leaders and innovators, I'd like to take a moment to talk about a significant new trend in educational leadership and innovation, particularly as we look back over the last year in review.

Clearly one of the hallmarks of great leadership, educational or otherwise, is the ability to think creatively and use technology creatively. This means, among other things, to be able to see—or make up—the connections in seemingly disparate elements, and to do a lot of shopping at Sharper Image.

It's a holographic universe out there, people, in case you didn't get the memo. We need to be like the Safeway store in Bowie, Maryland, that had an aisle marked Books and Socks. (This is absolutely true.) The creative whimsy of the minds at that Safeway knew intuitively that there were people who would go to an aisle specifically to get a new pair of socks and, while they're at it, pick up the new Stephen King novel.

The ability to weave connections among apparently random and isolated things is more than mere mental froufrou. It makes us more resourceful, gives us more options in any given situation, is at the very heart of creativity and humor, and lets us mix stripes and plaids with impunity. This ability is actively cultivated in some disciplines. There is, for example, an exercise in some playwriting classes that requires you to write a scene that integrates a number of isolated elements into a complete and comprehensible whole. One I recall required you to create a scene involving a man digging in his back yard, a set of keys, and a newly ordained minister. Go ahead. Think about that combination and try to fit it together into a story that makes sense. You could do this and similar exercises in your classroom.

This line of thinking and input from my friend Lynell has led me to create a new pedagogical approach that I'd like to share. I call it the Flea Market School.

I model my school after the fabled San Jose Flea Market, in San Jose, California. If you're ever in San Jose, you really must go to this place; it's a remarkable exercise in quantum connections (check out its Web site at www.sjfm. com). This flea market is what every flea market dreams of growing up to be, as it hears tales of life in a flea market economy. It's eight miles of stuff. It has its own map. It's so large it's got street names; booths there actually have addresses, and the owners can give you a business card with their business name and address on it. It has the largest farmers' market in the state of California, on Produce Row. It has live music. There's a barbershop. There's an amusement arcade. There's a full-size old-fashioned carousel. There are two playgrounds. There are 25 restaurants. There are ATMs. There are 2,000+ sellers. There are no fleas.

And there's stuff. Unimaginable stuff. Wantonly disparate kinds of stuff, nestled comfortably next to each other, as if the universe had chosen this place as a good spot to just dump its cosmic bric-a-brac into a kind of museum of its leftovers that you can buy at really good prices. I've grown fond of strolling through it, just to soak in the sheer complacent discontinuity of it. And to buy socks and books.

Along almost any given street in the San Jose Flea Market you can see an assortment of such things as: boots, tires, suitcases, watches, shampoo, toys, summer clothes, home stereos, Swiss army knives, pruning shears, comic books, power miter saws, lawn chairs, winter clothes, statues, aquariums, gloves, religious supplies, auto upholstery, silk flowers, lamps, Egyptian art, music CDs, wigs, TVs, baby clothes, paintings, bicycles, jewelry, bedroom furniture, camping equipment, sunglasses, birds, underwear, wallets, computers—the list is virtually inexhaustible.

So why not take the concept of a flea market and pedagogically apply it to the classroom? How much more creative and fun it would be to have students walk into a learning environment that careens from topic to topic with seeming recklessness, then to stop and seriously explore the links among them all.

"Today, class, we're going to discuss the Enlightenment from the point of view of John Lennon's song 'Imagine.' Then we'll talk about blowing milk bubbles through your nose, how and why. Next we're going to discuss Moore's Law and why Moore was recently forced to retire from the board of Intel and the ramifications of that action on recent religious observations in Madagascar. We'll explore the humor and musical technique of Victor Borge, and wrap up with an experiment on volume and pressure from both a physics and metaphysics point of view. At the end of our course, you will have tied all these elements, and more, into a single holistic and sensible project and portfolio."

Let's see. This, or teaching to a standardized test? Hmm, give me a minute. Yes, one is perhaps a good deal more challenging than the other. Isn't education supposed to be challenging, in a positive, creative, supportive way, no less for the teacher than for the student? People are typically pleasantly surprised at how well their imaginations work when they play with making connections: It is genuinely fun, and it always leads to more learning.

And speaking of learning, I need to go see if I can find a ferret at the flea market.

How the Facts of Learning Sank the FAQs of Scripting

It was ugly, that celebrated meltdown of classroom scripting we've all heard about. I know. I was there.

You remember, of course, how scripting began to infest our schools. Someone decided that what teachers needed was an exact, word-for-word script of what to say and do in the classroom. A few companies made a mint creating these scripts, which were used in many school districts, most notably the Los Angeles Unified School District. I guess they figured with all these new teachers coming in with so little training and experience, brought in to fill the huge demand for teachers, there had to be some way to ensure uniform quality (an ironic term for this approach) of teaching.

What better way to do that than to create a script that guided the teacher through every step of what to say and do? So the scripts said things like, "Hello, my name is [insert name here]. Today we're going to learn about the periodic table of elements. You will note behind me on the board [turn and point to board] …" And so on. Every word, every gesture, every step was thoroughly scripted. This was considered cutting-edge pedagogy.

It was all unbelievable nonsense, of course, and it was destined for disaster. It was the iceberg, and the classroom was the Titanic. I was at the bridge when scripting hit the 'berg.

I'm a reporter for the "World Global Enquirer," the classiest of the education tabloids. (We're the people who broke the story about the two-headed talking cow that was caught teaching in a Nebraska school. The uproar over that story was incredible! People couldn't believe how much better the students in that classroom were testing.) Anyway, even at a classy periodical such as ours, there was disbelief at the news about scripting. Being the paper's ace reporter, I was naturally assigned to get the real story.

I slipped into a crowded L.A. classroom one day and witnessed the scripting meltdown. A harried teacher on autopilot stood at the head of the room, script in hand, and started.

"'Good morning, class,'" he began in a stuttering monotone. "'How are all of you? Isn't it nice to begin our class with such pleasantries?'" He flipped a page and looked for his place on the next one.

Before he could start again, a student in the back of the room raised his hand. "Yo, teach!" the kid yelled.

The teacher entered first-stage panic. The iceberg could be heard scraping metal.

"Um …" the flustered teacher muttered. "We … um … will now begin to study …"

"Yo, teacher dude!" the incommodious student in the back shouted. "I have a question, and I need personal guidance on my educational journey of discovery." There were barely contained giggles and snickers from his peers.

The teacher wrestled with his Prime Directive—veer not from the script—and the immediate demand for his attention. He took another stab at following the script. "'… to study the wonderful world of quantum physics,'" he said. "Um … Let's begin with … "

"Yeah, but dude," the student interrupted. "I really need a drink of water and help with my existential dilemma."

"Yeah, me too," supplicated another student, sensing a delightful crisis unfolding.

"Um … let me just check something," the teacher said. He flipped through pages of scripts, desperately looking for something that would address this situation. "Ah!" he suddenly said. "Here we go: 'Students, if you have questions, let me refer you to our FAQs section.' You know, Frequently Asked Questions."

"Oh, you have all the FAQs of life right there in your book?" queried the first student.

"OK, how about this one: Do we exist objectively, irrespective of the perceptions of others, or are we merely the subjective projections of each other's egos and eccentricities?"

"Um …" the teacher responded. "Let me just see …"

"So, to put it another way," the second student said, "if we fell in a forest and there was no one there to hear us, would we make a sound?"

"Well … hold on …" the teacher said, continuing to flip pages frantically.

Emboldened by these developments, another student asked, "And what is the area code for Missoula, Montana? And is time merely the product of physical rotation of astronomical bodies, or does it exist also as an encoded perception of the human psyche?"

"Well …" the teacher responded. "The FAQs in my script book don't really cover those questions … I can give you an answer to 'Could you repeat your remarks about that last point?' And also to 'Would you please move a little to the right? I can't see the board.'"

"Yes, but those aren't our frequently asked questions," student one replied. "All day long, as we play our video games, listen to music with the bass turned up so loud it stuns small animals at a range of 50 yards, meet each other in online chat rooms, we ponder questions such as, 'Is the salutation "dude" still relevant to us today, knowing as we do its etymology as first a surfer's expression in the '60s and then its vogue as a catchphrase of the neo-flower children of the '70s and '80s?' Many of us feel the term can be used as we see fit, that it isn't prisoner to the meanings of its previous lifetimes. Others feel that it's an unnecessary and limiting throwback. What do you think?"

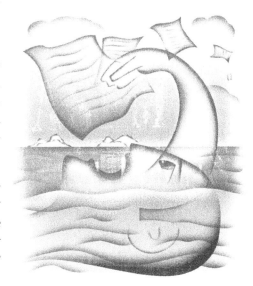

"But …" the teacher said. "Here's a very nice FAQ that I'm sure you'd enjoy: 'Excuse me, Mr./Ms./Mrs. insert name here, but would you please go over our reading assignment once more?'"

"I have a question," another student offered, riding the wave. "How does what we're supposed to be learning here today relate in any way to our real-world exigencies?

Can you give any example of how I'd be walking down the street, say, and see a cat trapped up a tree and apply my knowledge of quantum physics to that situation?"

"But … but …" the teacher repeated. The Titanic was heading for the bottom.

"And I have a question," student one said. "How are we to feel confident in our education when we have a teacher standing before us who is presenting nothing of his own personality and insight, but rather merely serving as a live recording of prepackaged information? Why are you even here? Why don't they just show a video of someone standing and reading the same stuff?"

"And what does this tell us," student two continued, "about how the system of education regards its teachers, and, for that matter, us? They're saying, we don't trust teachers to teach in any way except how we tell them to. And they're saying, students don't need the interactivity and individual character of the person who's supposed to be teaching them; they'll learn from a script whether they like it or not. I mean, where's the human connection, the personal touch in learning? Is that question in your FAQs?"

The consternated teacher paused, then slowly closed his script book. He tossed it to the floor. "No," he answered. "That question isn't in the FAQs. But it should be, in an FAQ document for the people who contemplate and then try to implement such things. All right, class, we're going out to do some real research. *A Beautiful Mind* is playing down at the second-run theatre. Let's go."

The insurrection had begun. And it continues.

Aisle Four: Frozen Food And Education

I'd had a good year, and I don't mean tires. I'd sealed a new deal for the school for celebrity endorsements, invented 19 new classes and repaired the loose banister in Barrett Hall. I was ready for something new and exciting.

It came, as so many opportunities do, in the form of a knock on the door, in this case the one to my office. I swung it open. There stood a pair of men looking like nothing so much as farmers trying hard to look like businessmen. They wore overalls under ill-fitting suit coats, with ties in knots big enough to hide a small rodent. Having had the benefit in years past of exhaustive military intelligence training, I concluded at once that these men were not my students.

"May I help you?"

One pulled off his knit cap. "Well, sir," he drawled, "we think maybe we can help each other."

"'At's right," the other mumbled.

"See," the first said, "we're farmers turned businessmen. We don't quite have the dress down, but we cut slicker deals than a pandering congressman. We got us an idea that's gonna make us richer'n our last one."

"And how rich was that?" I asked.

"You heard of Festering Farms Chickens?"

"Of course."

"That's us."

I was impressed, but perhaps not in the way they had anticipated. "Gentlemen," I told them, hoping the term would not confuse them, "perhaps you want our horticultural department. It's back up that way ...."

"This has nothin' to do with culture," Farmer A said. His friend snickered loudly at the idea. "No, sir. This's got to do with distributed learning."

Suddenly he had my attention. Only minutes earlier I'd been toying with new ideas for this very topic. I'd been in midthought about a CD-ROM serialization of the Battle of Thermopylae, intercut with scenes from *The 300 Spartans* when the farmers had knocked on my door.

"What did you have in mind?" I inquired.

"Look at it this way," said Farmer B. "Nobody knows how to package and ship stuff better'n us. You know them knockwurst and cauliflower breakfast patties you buy at the store?"

"My favorites," I lied.

"We load those right on the truck at our plant up the road. Shipped right from us to you."

Farmer A jumped in. "And that parsnip 'n' pork rind ice cream? That's ours, too."

"I believe you," I assured them.

"So Mel and me was thinkin' the other day. We heard about this distributed learning stuff from students at your school who work in our plant. How all it is is a bunch of learning that's just distributed from a packing plant like this school out to customers."

"Some students from our school are working at Festering Farms?"

"You bet. We got one from your economics class who counts eggs."

"Got another from political science we use to keep raccoons from expanding their hegemony into the chicken hutch. Even learned that word from him. Means building hedges."

"Yeah," ventured Farmer B. "So we're figurin', well, heck, we can do distribution. Don't nobody pack and ship better'n us. All we need is some learning to distribute."

"And that's why we're here."

"Yeah. You got any learning we can pack on our trucks? We'll cut you a heck of a deal."

"You know, it doesn't have to be something you did today. We figure learning doesn't gotta be shipped that fresh."

"It ain't like chickens."

"Yeah," said the other farmer, again starting to snicker. "I never heard of anyone gettin' salmonella from stale learning."

"Now, we know what you're wondering: Sure, these here are two dynamite business minds, but do they know technology?"

"Uncanny," I said. "The very words were about to leave my mouth. This is a high-tech school. We do technology-based education."

"'Course you do. Well, ain't nobody more up on technology than Festering Farms."

"I give up," I said. "How's that?"

"We've identified several new computer viruses."

"You got your Saddam Hussein virus, for example," the other one said. "Won't let you in any of your programs."

"Related to education, you got your Federal Budget virus. Keeps promising to give your system better resources and keeps diverting them to other devices."

"And how did you happen to discover these viruses?" I inquired.

"We found out that one of our chickens was a hacker."

"Caught her pecking on the keyboard one morning, sending e-mail, checking the stock market online."

"So we secretly watched her a while and saw her writing these virus programs."

"Gentlemen," I interjected, "I don't suppose you considered the possibility that she was just writing chicken scratch."

They looked perplexed at the thought. "Well, we'll never know," one said. "She's probably on a dinner plate in Muncie by now."

If these guys were any less astute, I thought, they'd need to be watered twice a week. Still, I was intrigued. Sure, these were simple, unassuming folk, but sometimes, I recalled, the best ideas come from little-used minds. I was ready to explore some possibilities. "Come on in, gentlemen. Let me show you what I've got in development. You tell me if you get any packaging thoughts."

Within just a few hours I was enthralled as it became clear we were poised to revolutionize distributed learning. We had some freeze-dried education ready to bundle with premium poultry, set to ship to supermarkets near and far. Buy a package of thighs and legs and get a CD-ROM on the literary merits of Chicken Little. Buy a frozen souvlaki dinner and get my new CD-ROM of the Battle of Thermopylae. We bundled some quantum physics material with a new yet-unnamed foodstuff the boys were creating from leftover fodder that had come into contact with hazardous waste spillage. We were walking on the brave new border of learning distribution, down Aisle Four, Frozen Foods and Education.

Net Trek, Episode One: Voyage of the Browser

Stardate 2010.4.1. This is Captain Rocky Goodlearner, commanding the United Space Ship Browser on its multiyear mission to boldly go where few global distance learning programs have gone before. We'd just finished refitting at some dot-com and were enjoying some badly needed time off. But it wasn't to last long. Suddenly, an urgent voice sounded over the speaker in my quarters.

"Captain," the voice said, "this is First Officer Jimmy Techno. We have ... situation."

"What is it, Jimmy?"

"Well, it's a kind of set of circumstances in which one finds oneself—"

"Jimmy, I know what a situation is. What is the situation we're in at the moment?"

"I think you'd better see for yourself."

"On my way."

There was near panic among my officers as I stepped onto the bridge.

"Report," I commanded.

"Sir," said my Technology Coordinator with his typical dry precision, "we're being pulled into a strange unplotted quadrant of the Internet. The helm is not responding."

"On screen."

The image that came up told the story. We saw the exterior of our ship, what some outsiders call a computer, with its power conduit disconnected. I quickly made an executive decision. "Somebody get out there and plug us in," I directed. Within moments we were humming again. I checked over our charts and gave the command to prepare for departure.

"What's our mission this time?" Jimmy asked me.

"We're to explore all sites related to distance learning for a 4th grade class in Upper Padoka, North Dakota, including all relevant rubrics and standards correlation information. And on the way back we have to pick up some milk and eggs."

"I could use some paprika, now that you mention it."

"Fine. I want you to check the dilithium crystals before we get underway. We can't have our fuel run out on us."

"Aye, sir," he said, and disappeared to complete his tasks.

I called to Chuck Netscape, our Navigator. "Navigator Netscape, how is the crew responding to the fact that we're going to be exploring the Internet without using an Internet explorer?"

"I think they've come to understand that here on the U.S.S. Browser," he answered, "it's we who are the Internet explorers—not the tools we use."

"Well put, Navigator. How's your brother doing in his new position?"

"He's very proud to be called Netscape, Communicator, sir."

"Good. All right. Give me a course."

"Aye, sir. First, I thought we'd move through the McRel quadrant to visit strange new alien worlds of standards correlation. Right after that I figured we might catch the double feature at the neighboring Net drive-in. Then it's off to the Curriculum Galaxy, probably the least explored area of Internet education, where we will be faced with tough content and delivery questions at every turn. Then we

visit the mysterious alien world called Rubrics' Cube. Finally, we swing through an online grocer and we're home."

"Make it so," I said.

Within minutes, we were underway. But almost immediately, the ship's warning system began to flash a Mauve Alert. "What's happening?" I shouted over the ship security speakers blaring, attention-getting country music.

"Cling-ons approaching from the north 40," my Security Officer Woof said.

"Open a channel," I ordered.

"We are the Cling-on Empire," a sinister voice informed us over the inter-ship communications channel. "We cling on to non-technological ways of learning that have worked so well for nearly a century, and we will challenge all those who attempt to pass through our mindset. Our system ain't broke, so to speak, and doesn't need your meddlesome fixing. Stand down and prepare to be boarded."

"We are on a peaceful mission of learning and friendship," I said, "and to pick up some groceries. We mean you no harm."

"There's a Safeway site a couple of clicks over," the Cling-on captain said. "You may have safe passage there, but if you attempt education destinations, you will be attacked."

"And why should we fear your attack?" I boldly challenged.

"Take care with your tone, puny human," the voice retorted. "We have the full force of social inertia at our disposal. Do not underestimate the power of apathetic complacency on full phasers, especially when voiced in a public forum."

I considered his words. Theirs was indeed a significant power, to be sure; they had defeated innumerable educational initiatives previously and were widely feared. But I knew too that it was time to take a stand, to stare into the face of the old order and win it over.

"We will not stand down," I told him. I could sense the chill my words sent through both the Cling-on captain and my own crew. "We are moving to Rubrics' Cube. Come with us and discover for yourself the joy of online education."

"Fool!" he responded. "Even if we were to allow you to proceed there, your fate would be the same as all before you: you would find yourselves constantly turning around in ceaseless circles, unable to solve that most challenging of all puzzles."

"Perhaps. Nevertheless that is our destination. Join us. Together we will solve the rubric riddle."

"Enough!" he shouted. "This discussion is at an end." Suddenly the Cling-on ship was on the move.

"Captain!" Officer Woof cried. "Their forward weapons array is powering up. They're preparing to fire their combined inertia-apathy beam!"

"Evasive maneuvers," I ordered. Instantly the ship began moving in a serpentine path.

"Impact in three seconds!" someone shouted, and indeed seconds later the ship was rocked by a bone-jarring explosion. Suddenly the way we were going somehow seemed good enough, and I just didn't feel as strongly about it.

"Shields are at only 30 percent power, Captain," Jimmy Techno told me. "Not that I really care."

I fought to shake off the crippling don't-give-a-darn sensation. "Forget the shields," I ordered. "Full power to the people. Protect the crew!"

"Captain!" a voice shouted from the engineering department. "Our dilithium crystals are destroyed! We're dead in the water!"

"Replace them with Folgers crystals! And release them throughout the ship!"

The ship jarred back to full power. Moments later we were able to jump to a link that set us spiraling away from the Cling-ons and off to a safe site.

"That was a close one," Jimmy said.

"Yes," I had to agree. And there will be more encounters as we pursue our mission. But at least it's becoming less a battle of wills than a disagreement over tools and procedures. The universe is moving to new understandings, new visions, which may be shared with all. It is indeed a bold new world into which few have gone before!

"Now let's get moving. I've got an online creative writing class to get to."

Tonight's Episode of "School Improvement"

Does everybody know what time it is?"

"TECH TIME!!"

"That's right, and now here's the host of 'Tech Time'—Tim Talon!"

"Thank you, Lisa, and thanks to all of you in the studio and watching at home. Yes, it's time again for everybody's favorite school improvement TV show 'Tech Time,' where we bring you the latest and greatest in educational technology. Why, if one were writing a humor column on this topic for an education technology magazine, one could say it was all about the Joy of Technology! Here at 'Tech Time,' we bring you technology projects you can do right in your own school to make your life easier—and, of course, more powerful, with lots of extra horsepower.

"And you all know my assistant, Al Moribund, right? Al, come on out!"

"Hi, Timmy. Did you tell the folks what today's project is?"

"Just about to, Al. Today, all you educators out there, we're going to show you how to set up and install your own wireless LAN."

"That's local area network."

"They know what it is, Al."

"Just trying to be helpful, Tim."

"If you really want to help, why don't you wear something besides flannel one day?"

"Very funny, Tim. Now, in setting up your LAN, you want to start with considering how much of an area you're going to need to cover. Do you want to reach your whole campus, or just a certain area of it?"

"Like maybe just your hippocampus."

"Unlike Tim, I'm being serious."

"So am I, Al. See, the hippocampus is an area of your brain —"

"Quite possibly the only one Tim uses."

"Good one, Al. The point I'm making is, when it comes to your LAN, use your head. Why settle for a plain old LAN when you can have one that's adrenaline-charged with 800 horses under the hood and a super V-8 engine with twin turbo exhausts and dual processors running at a cool five million functions per second?"

"Tim, do you have any idea what you just said?"

"I don't have to, Al. I just rattle off the features; I don't have to make it work. That's why I have an assistant, like you."

"Yep. Sounds just like a school system, all right."

"But actually, I do know how to beef up technology—that's what I live for. And what Al doesn't know is that I went back to the school where he just installed a nice little LAN and tweaked it a tad."

"What? You messed with my nice little LAN?"

"No, Al, I tweaked it. It was all pretty and safe and did what it was supposed to. I have two words to describe that: bor-ing."

"And I have three words to describe what happens when you tweak things, especially 'just a tad': hos-pi-tal."

"And you call yourself a tech tool man! Where's your spirit of innovation, of forging on, of damn-the-manual-full-speed-ahead? Anyway, it's already done, and I think we're going to be very pleasantly surprised with the result."

"I think I'd better call my mother and tell her to leave the city."

"Well, let's start this puppy up. Al, why don't you just push that button right there."

"I don't think so, Tim."

"This is where a leader has to step in. Now, watch your screen when I push this button, and you'll see the school light up with the glow of connectivity. And … now!"

"Wow. Would you look at that. I have to hand it to you, Tim. The school did indeed light up. Now, will that glow start to peel the paint after a while? And is there any radioactivity danger here? And are you supposed to be able to see through the walls like that?"

"All progress has occasional setbacks, Al. Well, the kids will be pleased while the school's closed, anyway."

"With all that extra light, I guess you could say you've successfully extended the school day."

"Got your point, Al, and a darned funny one it is. Let's move on to another project. Now, everybody knows that the most cherished institution in the cherished institution of education is standardized testing."

"That's what all the kids are saying."

"Well, we here at 'Tech Time' have developed a cool new way to do standardized testing."

"Who is this 'we' you speak of?"

"You ended that sentence with a preposition, there, Al. Remember what

Churchill said about that rule: 'This is something up with which I will not put.'"

"Didn't he say that about standardized testing, too?"

"Sure didn't, Al. Now, we all know that the challenge with standardized testing is making sure every school gets high enough scores so that the principal doesn't get fired."

"Well, that and the fact that it changes the focus from real learning to administrator job security."

"Let's not nitpick, Al. So we've developed a technology that absolutely guarantees high test scores! Working closely with the people at the largest online service in the U.S.—yes, I'm talking about AWOL—we've come up with an automated e-mail system that does e-mail automatically."

"Hence the term 'automated e-mail'?"

"You're a quick study, Al. Now, all of you at home are wondering what automated e-mail has to do with standardized testing."

"And what else is on TV right now."

"What we and AWOL have done is created homework e-mail that gets sent automatically to every student in America who has a standardized test coming up! But wait, there's more! Every e-mail comes packed with all the information any student would need to ace any test! It's fun, it's easy, and I've tweaked it so that it elbows all your other useless e-mail, like any from family and friends, out of the way!"

"That's really exciting, Tim."

"Now you're in the spirit, Al."

"What you don't know, though, Tim, is that the other 'we' here at 'Tech Time' have known about your automated e-mail plan for some time, and we've developed an effective antidote to it before it even gets started."

"What?"

"Well put, Timmy. Our software intercepts your automated e-mail and instantly replies to it, without the original e-mail ever hitting a target computer."
"Is that so?"

"It is. Would you like to know what gets sent back to the people sending all this automated homework e-mail?"

"Not really, Al."

"Country music song titles."

"You're pulling my leg."

"That's not one of the songs, Tim, but that's a good effort. No, I'm talking about timeless classics such as, 'At the Gas Station of Love, I Got the Self-Service Pump.'"

"You're kidding."

"I'd never kid about anything this serious, Tim. These are actual, real country song titles. Like 'My Wife Ran Off With My Best Friend, and I Sure Do Miss Him.' And 'How Come Your Dog Don't Bite Nobody but Me?'"

"How can you do this, Al?"

"Then there's my personal favorite: 'You're the Reason Our Kids Are So Ugly.'"

"You're knocking some serious work here, Al."

"No, I'm not. Through this we're celebrating the creativity of American country songwriters."

"I was talking about standardized testing. Well, that's our show for this week, folks. Keep studying, kids!"

"Keep writing new songs, kids!"

Live at the Interstate Internet Lounge

Let's face it, I thought to myself (as opposed to thinking to someone else). I'm lost.

I'd been cruising the Information Superhighway all night. I'd heard all the warnings about making sure you pull over and rest when you're tired, about how the road starts to blur into poor-resolution matrices after a few hours, about how you have to be careful where you pull off because of potential predators who may appear out of nowhere when you're too beat to think straight. I'd heard it all, but I didn't listen. Now I was beyond fatigue, well into catatonia, and not only did I have absolutely no idea where I was, but I'd even forgotten where I was trying to go.

My Fiat Pentium VIII was wheezing almost as much as I was by the time I pulled it over to the side of the desk. I rubbed my eyes and took another look at my windshield ... er, monitor. It was misting from a heavy predawn dew. Best I could figure, I was somewhere in the vast midwestern plains of the Internet, right around where you find sites for places like Bucky's Cheese Warehouse and Acme Screen Doors.

Suddenly a pair of headlights backlit my screen. I heard the crunch of braking microchips as the Internet Traffic Police vehicle approached me. Moments later I saw the officer's e-mail demanding my registration and serial number.

"What's the problem, officer?" I asked as I transmitted the information to him.

"Do you have any idea how fast you were going back there?"

he wrote back.

"Well, my modem is only a ..."

"I'm talking about how fast you were going in a bandwidth speed limit area."

"Oh." I had to admit I hadn't a clue, but I wasn't eager to tell him that.

"So, where's the fire?" he wrote.

It suddenly came back to me. "Well, see, I was in a hurry to get back to my classroom. I was vacationing this weekend, and I was late getting back. I'm supposed to be teaching a class in Internet and intranet applications first thing in the morning, and I ..."

"Save it for Internet Traffic Court," he interjected.

"What?! I can't do Internet Traffic Court! I don't have time!"

"Everybody's in a hurry, and nobody cares how they get there. You'll find time. Besides, you might learn something you can use for your class."

Then he was guiding my browser to the court site. It had that typical

governmental layout look to it, like someone had wallpapered a room with legal forms, taken a picture of it, then scanned it into an HTML document. At least it was over quickly. I pleaded guilty to contempt of bandwidth, and moments later I found myself in line to enter the Traffic School site.

"You have got to be kidding," I muttered as I double-clicked the site icon. Internet Traffic School was laid out like the lounge at the Lazy-8 Interstate Truck Stop down on southbound 5, where you can get a stale cheeseburger, a flat soda and a mind-numbingly obnoxious comedian doing his shtick, all for only $7.95. And the food was the better part of the deal.

It appeared the worst of the jokers doing the Lazy-8 circuit was also doing part-time gigs as an Internet Traffic School instructor. The SYSOP introduced himself as Davey Gawdy. His credentials included facility on both Netscape and Internet Explorer, a degree in e-mail protocol and two attempts to get booked on *Star Search*. And, of course, multiple appearances at the Lazy-8.

"Hey, hey, hey!" he shouted at us from Eudora Pro. "Who loves ya, people? Hey, I wanna give you all a great big warm welcome to Traffic School. Means a lot to me to have ya here. Hey, anybody here from out of town?"

"This is the Internet, Einstein," I wrote back. "We're all from out of town."

"Hey, that's right," he retorted, unperturbed. "And you know, in this crazy mixed-up, gotta-have-a-gimmick world, aren't we really all from out of town? You know, in a global village kind of way? Hey, you know, last night I played a blank tape at full volume, and the mime next door went nuts!"

"I hate to seem impertinent," I said, "but what does this have to do with Internet traffic?"

"You know, that's a good question," Gawdy replied. "No, actually, that's a great question. A timeless question. That's a question so profound it's an injustice to try to answer it. I, personally, who have performed at such distinguished venues at the South Bronx Traffic Court and Bucky's Cheese Warehouse Cafe, before mayors and tax adjusters, want to thank you for asking that." I could just about see him pulling a dirty handkerchief from the front pocket of his pale green lamé jacket and dabbing gently at his eyes. "But I digress," he continued. "Hey, what do you call a scared flower arranger? A petrified florist!"

On he went, a runaway train, a midnight express bound for oblivion and points west. Maybe, finally, that's what he had to do with Internet traffic, after all. Perhaps he was an annoying metaphor for the kind of congestion one must take pains to avoid as the lanes in cyberspace increasingly fill up with computers contracting electronic wanderlust. Davey Gawdy may have found some measure of redemption at last, as a road warning sign, the black silhouette of him guffawing at his own jokes prominent on a yellow triangle, telling us, "Turn back now. Before it's too late. Before, God help you, you end up on the Lazy-8/Traffic School circuit. Learn from such as I."

Here's to you, Mr. Gawdy. You're a unique Internet application, and I'm going to use you symbolically on my own inner intranet. You're a plug-in I can call upon whenever the urge to cruise that great invisible highway on the wire overwhelms me. With that thought, I pulled my tired Fiat back on to the main road. I felt like the Duke of URL as I entered my home page address. The one that would take me home, down country roads.

Mortal Assessment Versus Overlord of Algebra
Never let quality learning get in the way of making a buck

Well, it's a week now since Sayga Video Games announced its acquisition of the top educational assessment companies, and it seems like a good time to see how the deal is working out. I talked recently with Gil Bates, owner of Sayga and three-eighths of the Western world, about it.

Me: Mr. Bates, what made Sayga, maker of mindless, repetitive, noncreative video games, decide to pay big bucks for education assessment companies?

Bates: Well, it just seemed like a natural fit. Video games do nothing but sharpen eye-to-hand-to-wallet coordination. They dull creativity and learning, and many studies show that they actually cause a decrease in intellectual development. We were very inspired to see education adopt a process remarkably similar in its approach to assessment, particularly in standardized testing.

Me: I imagine you were.

Bates: Yes, well, you don't have to because I just told you.

Me: Well, clearly nothing gets by you. So you saw a kindred spirit in standardized testing and video games.

Bates: Exactly. Teaching to tests, forcing kids to be in a constant cramming state as a reactive reflex to misguided political pressure, posturing students' rote results to an unsuspecting public as proof of academic accomplishment—good gosh, we couldn't have invented a more sinister game if we tried.

Me: So I understand you're looking to make testing itself into a video game.

Bates: That's right. Of course, we didn't have to work too hard at it; there's so much really awful drill-and-kill software out there already that's great for our purposes. We just took some of those and reverse-engineered them to work as games in the classroom. We figure, what the heck, kids dread tests, so why not make them something fun? In addition to a grade score, why not be able to run up huge point scores that take you to higher game levels?

Me: Especially since they don't take kids to higher learning levels.

Bates: Well, there you go. We say, hey, that's just not right, darn it! Kids deserve more. They deserve to be able to take tests in a really cool Sayga game where they can get their name as high scorer.

Me: How many games are we talking about here?

Bates: Oh my gosh, the market is just huge! Lots of games here, you know, one for each class being taught, some for middle school, some for high school. The titles can go through the roof!

Me: What kind of titles do you have in mind?

Bates: As far as names go, we're playing with things like "Civics Death Match," "Overlord of Algebra," "Kung Fu Chemistry," "World History Drag Strip." The mind boggles!

Me: Mine sure does. And I hear there's a benefit of these games for classroom discipline, too.

Bates: You bet. Here's a good example. One of our top game developers, Zelda Benchpress, also happens to be a high-school teacher in a very tough neighborhood. She's developed a game based on an already popular game that she's modi-fied for her purposes. Now when kids face the prospect of being the "Prisoner of Zelda," it takes on a whole new meaning. They're drawn by the familiar name of the game they know, but once they're in detention, our Zelda makes them wish they could jump to another level very quickly.

Me: The old bait-and-switch, huh?

Bates: Well, I guess you could use that term. I'm really not very familiar with it, of course, coming out of the business world as I do.

Me: Of course. I'm sure the concept would be very alien to you. Well, how about the financial model for these games? How will that work out with Sayga owning the assess-ment companies?

Bates: It couldn't be better. I mean, the assessment companies were always about good business sense anyway. They never let quality learning get in the way of making a buck. Corrections to mistakes in the tests? These sharp business minds always knew that you can't make money by rewrit-ing tests just for the sake of accuracy; it's just too time intensive. Sure, some tried to farm the work out to cheaper labor in Micronesia and Tonga, you know, places like that that already have higher academic achievement than we do here. But these people always knew that the real money in education assessment is in keeping low information turnover—keep things simple, fast, crank student answers in and crank out high-visibility figures, don't get bogged down in what they mean or don't mean. The minute you have to do true assessment of true student learning, your financial model goes to hell in a handbasket, and handbaskets are expensive.

Me: I'm inspired.

Bates: Well, who wouldn't be? So of course this made assessment a highly attractive market for us to gobble up in yet another way. And we haven't even talked about professional development yet!

Me: Say, that reminds me, what about professional development?

Bates: Glad you asked. How many teachers do you know who know how to play a video game?

Me: You're saying there's not a lot of pinball wizards out there in educator land?

Bates: There may not be a more telling indicator of the cultural gap between student and teacher than level of expertise on a game handset. Well, if students are going to be taking tests on video games, teachers are going to have to know how to use them, too. You're going to see a lot of seminars and sessions on testing games. Watch for keynote speeches on better test gaming tips at conferences.

Me: So of course Sayga will have a booth at all the major conferences?

Bates: For sure. We're going to outspend everybody.

Me: I hear there's potential for spin-off marketing.

Bates: Sure. Look at classic games like "Super Mario Brothers" and "Mortal Kombat." Both of those got made into movies every bit as classy and memorable as the games they were based on. So we have every reason to believe that our new testing games will spin off into quality entertainment, too. It's one of the little side benefits that make being in this business so rewarding.

Me: So students could take a test game at school and that same evening see an engaging, spirited movie with endearing characters from the very test they took earlier that day?

Bates: Exactly. We'll just have to be careful not to put clues to future test answers in the story lines.

Me: Well, what about competition? I hear Sonny is hot on your heels with a special classroom gaming device called Test Station. Advance buzz on it is pretty hot.

Bates: They're trying to catch the wave, playing with some attention-grabbing titles like "Mortal Assessment." Sure, there's no question everybody's going to try to invade the market, sending games to school board members, trying to demonstrate that their games are best for standardized testing.

Me: Sounds like the testing game business is no game.

Bates: Very true.

Thinking Comes to College

When I got the word that we needed to acquire seamless integration of partnerships and collaboration in education, I knew where I had to turn. I was on the phone instantly with the Institute of People Who Think.

"Let me cut to the chase," I said in my typically no-nonsense approach. "You guys have a funny name."

"Thank you," responded the voice on the other end.

"No, I mean, what does the name really mean? Doesn't everybody think?"

"You'd think so, so to speak," the voice said. "But take a look around. Have you been on the roads lately? Have you watched a political debate? Have you examined a school budget? There's thinking and then there's thinking. We here at the Institute of People Who Think like to think that thinking is more than just ... well ... I think you see where I'm going with this."

"I never thought of it like that."

"Well, not to be rude, but that's why you don't work here."

"Point taken. So can you help me?"

"Of course. Oh, by the way, what's the problem?"

I proceeded to tell him what I needed. Our school needed seamless integration and we needed it yesterday. In moments, he'd set me up an appointment to come and meet with the high-powered minds at the Institute. They'd have a dizzying array of solutions for me to examine, he promised.

I arrived for my appointment and was immediately impressed. (These were not mere self-absorbed geeks with stratospheric IQs and too much time on their hands. They were also snappy dressers with a sense of humor.) They all wore tank tops with the word "Think" on them. "Get it?" one asked, nudging me gently in the ribs. " 'Think' tank tops? See, we're tops in think tanks …"

I was ushered into a conference room where the head thinker herself took some time to introduce the Institute's solutions. "It wasn't that long ago," she began, "that integration had seams. In fact, seams were all the rage back, say in the '40s. You had to have seams, and women were always trying to make sure they were straight. Today, of course, we know better. Seams are … well … unseemly."

This, apparently, was thinker humor, a real high-IQ knee-slapper, and the whole room went into a kind of controlled hysteria. I chuckled politely.

"So we've put our best minds into the question of seamless partnering in education. We have some real winners for you. Here's the first. Monty, why don't you do the pitch?" A square-shouldered gentleman with too-white teeth stepped up with something in his hand.

Monty was suddenly a used-car salesman, but he wasn't pitching cars. "Hey, folks," he began in a frenzied tone, "ever wish you could have that college degree you never finished? But you just don't have the time? Well, the fine people at Bother U. have teamed up with the Institute of People Who Think to bring you—" he paused long enough to hold up the object in his hand—"new College in a Can!" He was as excited as if he'd just won the lottery.

"Yes, it's College in a Can," Monty continued, "the new fun, easy way to get your degree! No more struggling to understand esoteric concepts mumbled by a teacher at the front of a classroom a light-year away! No

more of that mind-numbing schedule juggling and memory strain trying to recall where you're supposed to be next! No more homework, no more books, and no more teacher's dirty looks!

"You're saying to yourself, 'Monty, I've come to trust you; after all, you're the guy who told me about new Mosquito Condo, the best mosquito control device ever, which advertises great condo prices to mosquitoes moving into my backyard and then they buy it, but then get disgusted at the condo tax rates and decide to move to a cheaper back yard, only $39.95 from the Institute of People Who Think. 'But Monty, I don't understand why mosquito is spelled the way it is, or how new College in a Can works!' Well, let me explain!" You'd think Monty was announcing a cure for hangnails.

"College in a Can captures an entire college four-year curriculum into simple, easy-to-digest tablets. Just take one long-lasting time-release tablet each day and learn all day long! Imagine yourself at a movie some afternoon and suddenly becoming aware of the eschatological ramifications of dust bunnies. Or, making lunch one day, and suddenly understanding the difference between humus and hubris.

"College in a Can comes in a wide variety of majors, some of which you can even use later to make a living. And it's a fraction of the cost of a four-year college education!"

"Thank you, Monty," the Institute's head thinker said. She turned to me, astutely observing the confused consternation in my face, and asked, "So what do you think, so to speak?"

"You mean to say you actually have the technology to do this?" I asked. "And even if you do, doesn't this mean the end of colleges as we know them? Why would a college want this product to be marketed?"

She chuckled gently and patted my hand. "Such cute questions," she said. "Well, first, of course we have the technology. We've partnered—seamlessly, I might add—with the best cutting-edge minds in high-tech circles to make this possible. The tablets run on Linus 4.0 from Charlie Brown Software. Information condensing and encrypting is done by Hold That Thought from Hi Minds. The time-release technology comes from Penny Craig Weight Reduction centers and has the added benefit of helping you lose up to 25 pounds of unsightly fat within 30 days with absolutely no exercise or dieting!

"As for the marketing aspect—well, think about it for a moment:

who's going to provide all the content for College in a Can? Academia will enter a new Golden Age. And for those who might miss the social interaction of the classroom, we'll reposition colleges as College in a Can support centers, where you can go to dialog with your fellow canees with the very people who created the curricula."

"You mean to say that they'll still be college classes, just reframed?"

"Is that brilliant or what? Plus someone still has to do testing and hand out the actual degrees."

I was impressed. These people can think, I thought. As long as I was there, I took time to look at the Institute's new Pick-a-President product for streamlining the election process.I won't spoil the surprise for the elections this year, but don't be amazed to find Madonna appointed Secretary of Education.

The Story of PINokio

Once upon a time, in a school system far away, there lived a gentle and kindly old shoemaker and wireless device nerd. All day long, this beloved old man, whose name was Joe Petto, made and repaired shoes for mere pennies, and luckily he didn't need to eke out a living with his shoes because he was fabulously wealthy from his work with wireless handhelds and other cool techno toys. He just really liked shoes.

But Joe Petto was a lonely old techie, for he had no brood with whom to share his fortune, which was still quite large despite his stock holdings losing some 38 percent of their value. Every night he looked up at his wishing star high in the night sky (it was the satellite his company had put up to handle his wireless device traffic), and he made the same wish:

"Oh, wishing star and satellite in your optimal apogee, please let me one day have my own child with whom I may share my good fortune and a nice pair of patent leathers," he said.

Now it happened that Joe Petto had built a new wireless device, but this one was quite different from any that he—or anyone else—had ever made. For this wireless device was built in the shape and size of a young boy! Longing as he did for his own son, he had constructed the Walking Wireless device, the bold new frontier of wireless evolution, and he had created it specifically for education because he knew how much educators love technology and are always ready to embrace the new and exotic.

The Walking Wireless was just a prototype, still in testing, and it was designed to help education administrators with their harried workloads, despite its diminutive size and form. Already it could handle school e-mail and the full range of classroom management. It had powerful voice recognition software built in and artificial speech, too. Joe Petto had even conducted a spirited mock classroom discussion with the device, though he found it still crashed when it had to pass out standardized tests. He had named the machine PINokio, which referred to the fact that to use it you needed to enter your own PIN (personal identification number) and also referred to the company that had constructed the machine according to his design, Okidoki Enterprises. Those of you who write humor, such as accountants, will appreciate the lengths to which I had to go to make this name work for this story!

But while Joe Petto was very proud of his new creation, he was also sad, for he knew that he had built it like a boy because he so much wanted his own. Every night as he powered down the Walking Wireless device, he said the same forlorn words:

"Gosh, PINokio! Would that you were a real boy!"

Well, you will not be surprised to learn that Joe Petto had a Fairy Godmother, because this is a fairy tale, after all, much like the expectations placed on superintendents to raise test scores in the face of poor funding and insufficient public awareness of the testing process. Night after night, Joe Petto's Fairy Godmother had heard his plaintive pleading to his wishing star and his lonely longing to PINokio. So one night, the Fairy Godmother, whose name was something or other (I'm darned if I'm inventing another name), decided to help poor Joe Petto. She couldn't turn PINokio into a real boy—only his own true heart could do that. But she could make him operate without user interface or external power. She hovered over PINokio with her magic wand and blew a little fairy dust onto the Walking Wireless device.

"Wake up, PINokio!" she commanded it. "Wake up and walk!"

PINokio suddenly came to life and sat upright, even though his power cord wasn't even plugged in!

"I'm a true Walking Wireless device!" he exclaimed giddily. "No strings attached! But oh, to be a real boy administrator!"

"PINokio," said the Fairy Godmother, "Joe Petto is your father, and he loves you very much. He longs for you to be a real boy. But only you can make that happen."

"How can I become a real boy?" PINokio asked.

"Follow your heart and raise your test scores," the Fairy Godmother replied, "and watch your dreams come true!"

"You're sure I have to do both?" PINokio inquired, a little crestfallen.

"You've got two years," said the Godmother. "Piece of cake. And listen, ask Joe Petto if I can pick up my blue pumps on Tuesday."

Suddenly she was gone. But Joe Petto had heard all the commotion. He saw PINokio walking around without a power cord or batteries and was thrilled.

"Wow, the code I wrote must've been more powerful than I imagined," he considered.

"Not so, father Joe Petto," explained PINokio. "For it was your Fairy Godmother who brought me to wireless life, and left this claim ticket for her shoes. She says I can become a real boy administrator!"

"Then go forth boldly into The System, my son," Joe Petto said. "Reform education as I know you can, as I made you to do—and return to me a real boy!"

So PINokio got a gig as superintendent at a school with a very ambitious technology program. He got along very well with all the other appliances and computers, who admired him for his leadership and snappy circuitry. Well, almost all the others. There were two surly handhelds who were very jealous of PINokio and who hatched a plan to sell him to the circus, which was looking for an efficient way to order lion chow wirelessly. First they had to discredit his work at the school so he'd want to sulk away.

"You know, PINokio," said one of the handhelds to him one day, "you're really very good at your job, so this is hard to say. But you dropped your wireless signal in the office just now and didn't pick up this year's new technology plan!"

"No! No! It can't be!" cried PINokio, who was more than a little gullible—for Walking Wireless devices have pure hearts that can be easily misled!

"Can you be sure?" asked the evil handheld.

"Why … yes … of course, I can," said PINokio, though he knew it wasn't true. And at that very moment, his external antenna grew longer! Then he realized it would continue to grow every time he lied.

But just a moment later, he picked up a signal from his special friend Jiminy Rivet, assigned to help him by Joe Petto's Fairy Godmother.

"Follow your heart," whispered Jiminy. And by Jiminy, he did.

"You bad handheld!" scolded PINokio boldly. "Your behavior reveals why your company's stock value has plummeted! I will stay my course and never give up my dream of students acquiring real learning and education becoming the magnificent vessel of growth and wisdom it was always meant to be!"

"Bravo, PINokio!" exclaimed Joe Petto's Fairy Godmother, who had been watching. "You have followed your heart! Now you are a real boy!"

And so he was. He raised test scores while preserving real learning and so was able to keep his job. And PINokio and Joe Petto and Jiminy and all their students lived in their joyful classroom happily ever after.

Instant Staff Development in Good Taste

You see some pretty amazing things on late-night TV these days.

I was up in the middle of the night recently, tending to my colicky goldfish. When she finally calmed down, I decided to mellow out with a little mindless TV. I turned it on, and there on my screen was a man who looked like he'd been dressed by his mother—if his mother was a golfer, color blind and institutionalized. He was standing in a used-car lot in front of a huge pile of software. Balloons and banners behind him glistened in the sun, joyfully beckoning and conveying a sense that one would almost certainly be welcome to drop in on this place. A pretty young woman stood next to him; she was definitely not dressed by her mother, and she wore a banner that read, "I'm a teacher!"

"Hi!" she cooed to the camera. "My name's Joy DeVivre." I'll bet she teaches communications, I thought.

"That's right," the man interjected, talking as if he had a minute to live and had to say everything important to him as loud as he could. "And I'm Ernie 'Crazy' Selamander, and we're down here at the grand opening of the newest Doctor Cauliflower's Fast Food and Drive-Through Staff Development Restaurant." Now there's something you see every day, I considered.

"Hey," Crazy Ernie said, "how many times this week alone have you thought to yourself, 'Boy, would I love some cauliflower and I'd sure like to know what to do about staff development at my school?'" I hit six fingers contemplating his question before he interrupted. "Well, here at Doctor

Cauliflower's, we know making good cauliflower is all a matter of good education. That's why our cauliflower is Doctor Cauliflower. We have really smart chefs, the best minimum wage can buy, who use our secret recipe of 119 spices, minerals and trace elements to make mouth-watering cauliflower. Whether it's our new Barbecue Bacon Meringue Cauliflower or our longtime-favorite, Soy Jalapeño Peanut Butter Cauliflower, you can't do cauliflower better!"

"But that's not all, Ernie," Joy added joyfully. "Doctor Cauliflower's is also the only place where you get great staff development along with great cauliflower. Yes, now you can get credit for the seat time you spend while you're in the drive-through line. And what staff development you get!"

"That's right, Joy," Crazy Ernie said. "Nothing but the best. You'll get all the hottest training. The Case for Solving the Square Root of Pi. Whither Electricity? Helping Your First Graders Understand No Exit. Dressin' Hip for the Classroom. The Computer: Just a Large Electronic Pencil. Semicolon Cleansing: The Difference Between Grammar and Anatomy. Advanced Slang Among People Born After 1980. The Seven Pillars of Creating Presentations Based on Popular Numbers."

"And all our staff development training comes in cholesterol-free, low-fat discs that you simply download to your computer," Joy bubbled. "You also get a certificate you can proudly display next to your diplomas proving that you've received a genuine Doctor Cauliflower training—and that you can use for academic credit!"

"Yes, friends, you can put on valuable credentials without putting on one ounce of weight!" Ernie added. "Come on down today and ask for the Happy Teacher Meal!"

"But we've saved our most exciting news for last," Joy said breathlessly.

"That's right! Teachers, we're incredibly proud to announce our newest venture into instant staff development. Announcing—"

The scene suddenly changed. The camera now aimed at a luxurious velvet curtain with spotlights dancing randomly across it. A fanfare arose in the background.

"Ladies and gentlemen," Crazy Ernie said in a quiet, reverential tone, "from the city that gave you the quickie marriage chapel, the hometown of the fast and easy, the capital of convenience—it's the Doctor Cauliflower Quickie Staff Development Chapel, on the Las Vegas strip!"

The curtain parted to reveal a tiny chalet-like building on that famed Vegas street dwarfed by gigantic casinos behind it. A neon sign atop the building and almost as large flashed the inviting name of the establishment, just as Crazy Ernie had spoken it. By the magic of digital editing, Ernie and Joy now appeared at the building site.

"Hey," said Ernie with his characteristic Cole Porteresque delivery, "picture this: you're days away from some deadline for staff development, and there's just not a seminar or workshop anywhere on the calendar. You're going nuts! What'll you do?"

"No problem," chirped Joy. "There's always some course you can take instantly at D.C.'s Quickie Staff Development Chapel! We've cut the red tape so you can add credentials in the world's greatest playground!"

"Yes, teachers, now all you have to do is make one simple phone call, catch a plane, walk into D.C.'s Quickie Staff Development Chapel, and walk out minutes later with a certificate!"

"We provide the trainer!"

"We provide the flowers!"

"We provide the music!"

"And, friends, we're in Las Vegas. That means we can get the best staff development trainers in the world, right in our own back yard!"

"Imagine Siegfried and Roy teaching zoology and classroom fashion!"

"Picture Willy Nelson teaching music and tax preparation!"

"Wayne Newton giving a workshop on mustache maintenance!"

"Andrew Dice Clay doing a seminar on diplomacy!"

"And we make coming to Vegas ridiculously easy for you. Just call any travel agent and ask them for the Doctor Cauliflower Vegas Special." ·

"The special not only gives you the best teacher rates to Vegas.

You also get a bucket of chips you can use in any Vegas casino!"

"Call now!"

I was electrified. What a concept! It was about time someone took heart on the hard life of gaining academic credentials and bettering oneself for the classroom. I was on the phone in minutes, in Las Vegas in days, in a seminar on Better School Security offered by casino guards soon after, and in a casino dropping chips into beeping, blinking machines soon after that. I got to meet Crazy Ernie and Joy while there. They were all I'd hoped they would be.

Dearth of a Salesman

It was one of those steamy Sacramento nights when the fog rolls in off the Rio Grande like a shopping cart with a loose wheel. Yeah, okay, so I'm geography challenged. But an interesting metaphor, huh? Anyway, I was in my classroom, getting ready for the next day's assignments. An impertinent knock came at the door.

"Go away," I said graciously. (You should hear me when I'm in a foul temper.)

"Mr. Davis," came an annoyingly cheery voice attached to a similarly annoying face that appeared out of the mist in my doorway. "You are Mr. Davis, aren't you, Creative Thinking teacher? Sure you are. Can't mistake the face of a creative person."

"Right category, wrong person. I'm Barry Manilow."

"Love your music. Seriously, though, Mr. Davis, I'm here to help you."

"Whatever you're selling, I'm not buying."

"It's interesting you say that, Mr. Davis. I'm actually here to GIVE you something. The gift of a lifetime that will change the lives of you and your students forever."

"And it costs how much?"

"We can quibble over figures later. Mr. Davis, prepare yourself for a shock."

"You're leaving?"

"Sir, I'm prepared to give you an absolutely outrageous deal on previously owned educational technology!"

"Excuse me?"

"And I've also got some terrific vacuum cleaner bags, but I'll come back to that. Yes, you heard me right. I've got unbeatable bargains on technology just a split second behind the most current. But it'll get done what you need done, at a fraction of the cost."

"Okay, I'm caught in morbid curiosity. Give me your spiel."

"Sir, this is not a spiel. It is an ode to efficiency. Okay, say you want to teach your students how to read."

"Curiously, that actually happens to be on most educators' agenda."

"There you go. Well, I've got a nifty little number for you that'll help do that very task. It's called a 386, with some reading training software dating back no later than '95. Maybe you remember that year? Microsoft actually named a whole operating system after it."

"So I hear."

"Sir, this system was once used by Podunk Polytech for Kids. Brought it in for a trade-in. Barely used. Lots of miles left on it. I mean, just imagine the impact this kind of technology can have on your entire educational program!"

I studied the kid for a moment. He was like a lot of kids these days, eager, enthusiastic, short. Sure, he meant well, but it was time to give him a reality check. One that wouldn't bounce. "How long you been out in the field, kid?" I asked.

"Um, let's see, what's today? Well, altogether ..."

"Kid, what's the square root of pi?"

"Um, I used to know that."

"Quick, read this chart." I pulled down a chart I keep with happy quotes from Ambrose Bierce. He gazed at it quizzically.

"This chart, here?" he stalled.

"Where is Botswana?"

"Um, that way?" he said, pointing out the window.

"What's another word for synonym?"

"I ... I ..."

"Just as I thought. Look, kid, technology today changes every 14 seconds."

"Really?"

"I don't know. I just made that up. But it's really fast, that's my point. And it's already changed education enormously. Today, students have the capability to learn at a rate unheard of before. The best technology keeps up constantly with the increasing pace of learning."

"But I could really sweeten the deal ..."

"You're not listening, kid."

"I'll throw in 16 legs of lamb."

"That's megs of RAM."

"And an extra pair of pants."

"You know, kid, there are three kinds of people in this world. Those who can count, and those who can't. You're in that latter category."

"My synapses hurt."

"I'm not surprised."

I told him to have a seat, deciding it was time to take him for a demo run on my hottest new machine. I fired up my Fiat Pentium VIII, pointing out to him there was a reason a sports car company was now making computers. "Now watch him closely," I said.

"Who?" the kid asked.

"The computer."

"The computer is a he?"

"My wife says computers have to be male because they have a lot of data, but they're still clueless. I think they're female because even your smallest mistakes are stored in long-term memory for later retrieval. Anyway. Watch him closely." A nanosecond later the Fiat coughed up a test sheet from a recent exam I'd given the class. The grades of Winnie McKinney, one of my students, lit up the Fiat's screen. "Now, look at this guy's grades," I said to the kid. "Advanced alchemy, A+. Nuclear gardening, A. Power robotics, A+. Nautical psychometry, A-. That's his lowest grade."

"Wow."

"Well put. All of this possible through the magic of technology. New technology. Not that used stuff."

"Previously owned."

"Whatever. Many of these subjects didn't even exist an hour ago. Now we're creating whole new subjects, teaching them and grading them, in mere minutes."

"New technology can do all that?"

"I'm exaggerating a little. My point is, technology is the best teacher."

"I thought time was."

"Well, it is, but it kills all its students. Technology tends to be a little more disinterested in an afterlife, except as it relates to upgrades."

"Cool."

Well, in short time I had the kid finally understanding the deeper urgency of new technology and how it was changing education. He took a few laps with the Fiat and was on fire. When he came in he thought a quarterback was a refund. He confided in me that they'd had to burn his school down to get him out of the third grade. Now he was in a techno reverie, alit with the flame of advanced circuitry. He would peddle tired technology no more.

"Which way to the future, kid?" I asked.

"That way," he answered, pointing to the Fiat.

"'Atta boy."

As he headed out the door, full of certainty and confidence, a deep satisfaction came over me. I put on some Barry Manilow and invented some new courses, having to do with time travel and hollandaise recipes (separately, of course). I watched the Rio Grande fog clinging to the docks at Old Sac and for the first time wondered how it got all the way up here.

How the Schmall and the Marine Came to Schools

People always think the life of an education talent agent is all glamour and good times. Sure, the money's great, and you're in show business. But the job also puts your people skills to the test.

Take the time I was trying to work out a new contract for a principal in East Duluth.

The school was playing hardball and dug in their heels at four million five over three years. I knew my principal was worth $6.2 million, easy.

"Listen," I told the school's agent on the phone, "she's a three-time MVP, in both leagues, the AFT and the NEA. She took her school to six consecutive championship playoffs and one World Series of Education championship. That kind of talent don't come cheap." (We education talent agents sometimes like to use incorrect grammar to sound classier and more expensive.)

"Sure, she's good," the school's agent conceded, "nobody's saying she isn't. But let's be realistic. The school owners have to deal with a salary cap these days, and free agents like yours just keep getting pricier."

"Hey," I said, "you want to draw big attendance at

your school, you need big names. They cost money—you know, the stuff you have to spend in order to make some."

"Look, our salary cap is frozen at $16 million, with bonuses. We just can't afford her. No one can."

"Oh, really? That's not what Casper Elementary told me."

"What?! Casper Elementary's going after her? They haven't even appeared once on *Monday Night Education*! How can they afford her?"

"How can they afford not to have her? You might ask yourself the same question."

He whined another few minutes, but by the end of the conversation, we had our six point two. But that negotiation was a walk in the park compared to some more recent challenges. Take, for example, the trend toward selling school facility names to big corporations for big money.

In their never-ending quest for more partnerships and money, schools took a cue from sports facilities. Those have been selling names to corporations for years. There's Pac Bell Park. The Pepsi Arena. The Bridgestone/Firestone Racing Academy.

Now I was starting to get calls like this:

"Hi, I'm from a major tobacco company, and we'd like to talk with you about buying names of facilities of schools you represent."

"Excuse me?"

"For a very attractive price, one of your schools can have its own Marlboro College of Medicine."

"Who is this really? How did you get this number?"

Another time someone doing a bad Mel Blanc voice called and said, "Can't you picture it? The Elmer Fudd School of Diplomacy."

"Be vewy, vewy quiet," I replied, "and go away. We have too many politicians already who've studied way too many Looney Tunes."

Of course the trend didn't stop there. Companies wanted more than to just have their names on school buildings. They wanted a bold new kind of partnership that brought their very stores and products into the school's everyday life and curricula. Of course it's not unusual to find a fast-food shop in a college student union. This newer idea took that a huge step further.

"We're talking major draw into classes," one pitchman told me on the phone not long ago. "Kids love to shop anyway. I'm telling you, we put in a Sharper Image right next to the computer lab, and they'll pack the place. Why not hold fashion classes right in the middle of an on-campus Nordstrom? Have home ec right next door to a Sears. It'll be great! It's half school, half mall, all in one convenient location! We'll call it the schmall. They'll have names like the Target/Grover Cleveland Plaza and High School!"

"Better yet," another sales rep told me one day, "if you've got a school in a pricey area like, say, Silicon Valley, where ramshackle homes sell for over a million dollars, just sell the school buildings for a housing tract. You'll make a bundle, and then you could even pay parents $3,000 a household to homeschool their kids! Everybody wins!"

Then there was the time when every school on the planet had to have not just all-star educators, but big-name partners from the business and entertainment worlds, too. Talk about pushing salary caps to the max. I had all kinds of top names lined up, but I kept running into the same sad wall. Take this conversation I had not long ago with a rep from a school back East.

"Okay," I started out, "you're in luck. I got Ricky Martin available, exclusive to your school, to do music classes for only a mil five. He can be there tomorrow."

"Oh, man," the voice on the other end sighed, "no can do. I mean, he's boffo, and the price is good. But, man—music? Where've you been lately? Nobody's doing that gig these days."

"What're you talking about? Music's been making a big comeback in curricula around the country."

"Yeah, sure, but—"

"Well, hold on, I've also got Steve Jobs available to teach computing and playing well with other children."

"Pass."

"George W. Bush on media relations."

"Don't think so. Look, all these people are yesterday's news, dude. These days, if a major name can't help us deliver higher scores on our standardized tests, then they can't help us at all."

"Are you serious?"

"Hey, do you happen to know Judge Judy? She could order our kids to do nothing but study for tests. That's what we need."

"How about a nice tough general from the Marines?" I said facetiously.

"That's great! 'The few, the proud' can be our slogan for passing tests! And those who don't pass can leave school and enlist right on the spot! You're a genius!"

"I know, but I was also kidding."

Of course, this whole standardized test craze will die a well-deserved death none too soon, and students will actually start learning again and not just passing tests. But that craze has a nice side effect, though. When my education stars are suddenly needed again, fees will go through the roof. Hey, it's a living.

The Truth of Teen Talk

Don't let anybody ever tell you that kids today lack in creativity and artistic inclination. It is, in fact, so pervasive and subtle that it totally eludes mere adults.

I've recently completed an exhaustive study of the communication habits of teens (conducted over several hours of standing in line at the San Antonio, Texas, airport), and I am pleased to report the discovery of a kind of Rosetta Stone of teen talk. It demonstrates conclusively the stunning artistry that is carried in their seemingly obtuse language.

I should like to offer, as an example and in the lack of vast pages of appropriately prepared scientific data, which I really don't feel like writing, the following conversation I observed in the research facility identified above (airport code: SAT). I will show the actual words two high school-age teen girls on spring break used with each other, immediately followed by the decoded real meaning of their words.

Girl One: "Hey."

Decoded meaning: "I offer salutations in the manner of our kind, affording us an instant sense of community and camaraderie and at the same time effectively blocking understanding from any other sentient organism on the planet."

Girl Two: "Hey."

Decoded meaning: "Well met, friend, and I respond in like kind."

Girl One: "Like, would you believe?"

Decoded meaning: "We seem to be stuck in this line, which moves at a clocked speed of zero point zero zero three centimeters per century.

How rude and incommodious!"

Girl Two: "Like!"

Decoded meaning: "Verily! Astutely observed."

Girl One: "So, like, you got the things?"

Decoded meaning: "Understand that I am not challenging you; I merely wish to inquire whether or not you retain possession of our documents of transit."

Girl Two: "Duu-uuh."

Decoded meaning: "I mean this strictly in a spirit of jovial insouciance: of course I do, for were it otherwise I might incur castigation or doubt as to my ability to navigate the physicality of this world."

Long pause.

Girl One: "So."

Decoded meaning: "Perhaps we are well advised to view this delay as an opportunity to reexamine our station in life."

Girl Two: "Yeah."

Decoded meaning: "You intrigue me. How do you mean? Please elaborate."

Girl One: "Well, I mean, like, really."

Decoded meaning: "Regard, if you will, our present circumstances. We are as frozen amoebas, shapeless in our course, utterly immobile—and do not let the irony escape you that this occurs to us in the nexus of a facility intended to afford the most rapid transit possible today. Our physical immobility is but a lucid metaphor for the stagnation that occupies every level of our lives. Was it not Kierkegaard who once queried, 'A life lost in stasis is a life lost'? Truly we are in this world, but we are hardly part of it, for who welcomes us but our own?

Sometimes, I perceive, the universe sees us and emits a vast cosmic guffaw, mocking us in spite of the strife we endure in pursuit of our personhood."

Girl Two: "Okay, like, sure."

Decoded meaning: "How true! So it may well be that this very moment—us blocked from motion and direction, turned from egress to the life that lies ahead of us—indeed does reflect the ignoble circumstances of our time. But surely there is more in store for us than to be merely two psychic castaways eternally awaiting a Godot who never comes. Surely we may dare hope for individuation as we are drawn inexorably toward our generation's eschatological fulfillment! And I believe that quote was not Keirkegaard. I think it was Fournier."

Girl One: "Whatever."

Decoded meaning: "Who may say? Would that you were correct, about all but the quote! And indeed I suspect you are, if we may take meaning from the others that surround us here, the so-called adults. For while these people surely lack the spark and verve of life that we know and cherish, nonetheless we observe that they seem able to make their way, and some few may experience the joy of fulfillment."

Girl Two: "I am so sure."

Decoded meaning: "I'm not so sure. Have you observed our parents lately? Our teachers? Can you name any of these kind whose life you would want for your own?"

Girl One: "Like, okay."

Decoded meaning: "Your point is well taken. Still, there must be hope, for what else do we have?"

The conversation continued for hours, the pointedly monosyllabic nature of their words disguising the deeper levels of communication going on. Their discussion was powerfully touching, able as I was now to understand it. (I'm pretty sure this sudden capability was due to a combination of extreme fatigue and the effect of the aroma of some woman's perfume evidently applied with a paintbrush.)

I offer this to afford educators everywhere the chance to experience the true conversations of their students. Imagine the efficacy and immediacy of communication that can now occur in the classroom, as we converse with students in their own terms:

Teacher: "Hey."

Decoded meaning: "I don't wish to intrude upon your carefully drawn boundaries of community, young adults, but I wonder if I might have your attention."

Student (representative of the class): "Whatever."

Decoded meaning: "This is a disturbing development, that you are able to address us at our own level of communication. However, we will suspend judgment as to your intentions for a moment—only a moment, mind you. Say what you have to say, and we will decide whether or not to continue this dialogue."

Teacher: "Cool."

Decoded meaning: "I appreciate your gesture of openness. I shall endeavor not to abuse your generosity of spirit, knowing, as I do, how precious are your boundaries and how desperately significant is your quest for identity in a world you never made. Let us examine our respective situations: you are here, in many cases not because you wish to be. I am here, drawn as I once was to a calling which I believed could truly benefit those of your age and, thereby, the world at large. May we not choose to make the most of this? May we not elect to explore new boundaries, both of community and learning? If you wish, I will be your helpmate in this great adventure! I will respect your sense of quest. I will not force myself into your world, but remain nonetheless always at the ready to assist you when you need. I am, in the fullest sense of the expression, at your service."

Student: "Like, well, okay."

Decoded meaning: "Daring words, adult authority figure! Understand that if we choose to believe you and accept your proposal, it will be incumbent upon us to test your veracity at every turn—not out of some wanton belligerence, but because that is our station in life at this age. We will proceed on this joint sojourn, with the warning we have just issued clearly understood. Tread carefully, bold teacher! Our fate and our daring to trust are, in no small way, in your hands!"

This is the real artistry of our age: the capacity to comprehend the real language of those in our charge, and to appreciate the genuine artistry that they demonstrate in navigating their daily lives.

Home-School-Mall
Connection

I was in my office, perusing the new issue of *Educator Angler*. It's the one with the great list of fishing holes for best schools of fish (meaning fish with best practices in their schools). I was doing the crossword puzzle, looking for a four-letter abbreviation for "abbreviation," when it suddenly hit me. We're always in such a rush these days to condense things: books, processes, milk. Now even words, apparently. Nobody ever says, "Well, to make a short story long." No orator ever says, "Accustomed as I am to public speaking, I think I'll drone on for several hours."

I didn't like this direction. What we need, I thought, is more human contact and communication, not less. I remembered the last time I brought in some people from area businesses into my class. After only a few minutes, one of them said, "I don't mean to cut this short," meaning that he meant to cut this short, "but I'm late for my root canal." I had to spend a lot of time reassuring our food services people his remark was entirely coincidental to dining in the lunch room.

I was determined to create a bold new community involvement program for my school, one that would focus on real, in-depth communication and creative connecting, one that would span differences, bind us closer together as a human family and bring in a few dollars. So I set up an initial planning meeting with a bunch of community types. I had parents, of course, and students. I wanted to include area companies, and I was almost sure there were some. I did a lot of research, spending hours in a fascinating document filled with yellow pages and discovered there are actually quite a lot of different kinds of businesses beyond the borders of academia.

The night of the meeting, the place was packed. "I'd like to thank you all for being here," I said persuasively. "I'll throw the floor open to discussion. Feel free to bring up anything you feel is significant to both the school and the community. You there, in the back, dressed like a very large insect."

"Yo," the man began. "I'm from the new insecticide store, Doom Buggy." He turned, rather awkwardly in his costume, to the students in the auditorium. "I need some kids for our school-to-work program. Some interns. Are you kids studying bugs in school?"

My nerdiest student made me proud. "Sure," he said confidently. "I debug software programs all the time. It's really no different than rounding up your odd insect. I like to call my bug-killer program Motel Deep-Six. Bugs check in; check out time never comes."

The guy who looked like a roach on steroids and my nerd stepped to the side of the room to chat business. Then one of my teachers stood and addressed the crowd. "I started out in business," he said sullenly, "but I had it pretty rough. So I left business to go into education. Now, here at the school, I'm performing cutting-edge food science experiments, trying to determine the effects of mixing pasta and antipasta [sic]. So far it appears to be an explosive combination. Anyway, I need to find a new venue to test my experiments. I have a bold plan to propose what I think will solve several problems.

"I need a better testing laboratory. I need a location where subjects already like to hang out. I need ..."

"Yes. Yes. I see where you're headed with this," interrupted another man, jumping to his feet. "You need a food court at a mall. It's brilliant. What better way to maintain active community involvement with education than to combine schools with malls?"

A woman excitedly exclaimed, "Of course! A school mall. Classrooms right in the stores."

The bandwagon was rolling. Another woman shouted, "You can teach political science at Banana Republic."

"Home economics at Bed, Bath & Beyond," someone else shouted.

"Anatomy at Victoria's Secret."

A minor scientific problem occurred to me, as much as I hated to derail this train of thought. "But people," I said, "there's one major issue we'd have to fix."

"What's that?" someone asked.

"Well, you know how like-magnetic poles repel each other. That's the principle behind that powerful new means of travel you've heard about, based on the law that cats always land on their feet and the similar law that when toast drops, the buttered side always lands on the floor. So now they attached toast with the buttered side up on the backs of cats and then drop the cats. The two forces cancel each other out, and the cats simply float a few inches off the ground. They're setting up whole new rail systems using these toast-cat devices."

"So what's your point?"

"Well, here similarly, we'll have two competing forces at work. They might cancel each other out. On the one hand, there's the overwhelming propensity for kids to go to malls and stay there for lengths of time that defy even the outermost boundaries of quantum physics. Against that there's the equally powerful force that generates astonishing resistance in many kids to going to school. If we play these forces against each other, we could have enormous numbers of kids dotting the landscape for miles around, kids just stuck in space, unable to move in any direction."

It was a sobering reflection, and everyone put his or her mind to the problem. Long moments of silence reflected the depth of thought occurring. Suddenly the giant insect proclaimed he had the answer. "Well, who says we have to call it school?" he said. "We call it—a game. And it has its own theme song, 'Take Me Out to the Mall Game.'"

I had to admit it was brilliant, certainly the best thought to emerge from a man dressed like several species of bugs all in a single costume. We could see kids getting into going to games at the mall, with a little harmless learning going on at the same time. It was a superb example of how community involvement can really expand the horizons of education, and I urge you to do something similar at your school.

My Big Appearance on
Who Wants to Be
a Staff Developer?

You probably remember me. I'm the guy who appeared on that infamous episode of *Who Wants to Marry a Principal?* How was I supposed to know her school hadn't met minimal test score standards for the second year in a row and she was about to be fired? After that she went back to her first love, counting ladder steps on telephone poles. Well, I like excitement as much as the next guy, but it was clear that relationship wasn't going to work.

Yeah, my luck on TV game shows hadn't been all that great. But when I heard that *Who Wants to Be a Staff Developer?* was taping an episode in my town, I just couldn't resist trying out for the show. It was quite an experience.

"Okay, listen up, people," a surly voice said as soon as all 200 of us entered the studio that day. It came from the line producer, a brusque fellow who took no liking to academics. The feeling quickly became mutual. "First of all, let's get the ground rules straight. You'll all be asked to answer an initial tryout question. Whoever answers it right in the shortest time will then go on to play the actual game with our star. Any questions?"

"Yes," a voice from one of us said. "Why are we doing this?"

"It's the new approach to developing staff developers," the producer answered. "You're here because you all indicated that you wanted to become professional development professionals, if you follow me. Education's been trying to come up with a good system for developing staff development staff, and we decided to give this a shot. Early indications are that it'll not only work, but it'll also wipe out *CSI* in its time slot."

Soon thereafter we were corralled into the studio seats. Ten of us were randomly split off and seated in specially designed chairs with push-button devices attached to them. Then from the back of the room emerged the star of *Who Wants to Be a Staff Developer?* Tania Lightoff.

"Hi, folks," Tania said cheerily. "Let's begin the show, and we'll start with our first quiz to see who gets to come up here with me and play *Who Wants to Be a Staff Developer?* Everybody ready?" A rousing cheer of assent went up. "All right, then. Before we start, I want to remind the academic audience at home that all our questions are posited in the time-honored and tradition-bound way of our people: they're all multiple choice, of course, and correlated to national and state standards. And, they assess absolutely nothing about your actual intelligence or performance skills; they're simply designed to gauge your ability to commit to rote memory—and, hey, that's what passing tests is all about!" This, of course, was positively thrilling to as many as three or four of us.

"All righty, then," Tania continued. "Here's the first question. Arrange the following songs in correct chronological order: 'Early Morning Rain,' 'Tuesday Afternoon,' 'Monday Monday,' and 'Night Fever.'" A stupefied confusion seemed to settle over us as we pondered the question, and finally some overwhelming sense of rote came over me, and before I knew it (or the actual answer), I had won. Tania gestured to me and shouted, "Come on down and play *Who Wants to Be a Staff Developer?*"

There I was, in the hot seat, the big chair opposite Tania Lightoff on national television. I must admit, I was nervous. But I knew my business, and I was confident.

"Congratulations," Tania said. "Okay, get comfortable. Now, as you know, we start off with really easy questions for smaller prizes, and then the questions get harder as we approach the grand prize. And you have three lifelines, ways to get help, available to you as we go."

"Gotcha," I said.

"Okay, here's your first question, for a grant to buy office supplies. Who is buried in Grant's tomb? Is it a) Woodrow Wilson; b) Hugh Grant; c) Ulysses S. Grant; or d) Roy Rogers' horse Trigger? Take your time."

"Tania, I've got to go with my gut on this one. I'm going to say c) Ulysses S. Grant."

"Is that your final answer?" Tania challenged playfully.

"It is, unless the state of New York switched the body."

"And you're right!" Music swelled up and Tania looked at me like I'd just won the Nobel Prize. "All right, next question, this time for paint to redecorate the hallways of your school a calming shocking pink. Where is the capital of Paraguay?"

"Is this a trick question?" I asked.

"Well, sort of. Here's your choices: a) Montevideo; b) Caracas; c) Buenos Aires; or d) Paraguay."

"Tania, I'm going to with d), Paraguay."

"And you're right again! Boy, you're really on a roll!"

"I used to give multiple choice tests in my school."

"And doesn't the experience show?" An approving applause rose from the audience, and I felt sweetly appreciated.

"Now we move into the tough questions," Tania said, "and I think you'll see why when you hear what the next prize is. It's an application for a temporary waiver of certification as a staff developer!"

"Wow!" I said. "I take it that's one-time nonrenewable."

"Of course, with a requirement to obtain official certification within two years."

"Cool. Let's go for it."

"All right. Here's your question. When a positron passes its neighboring electron to scoot quickly into the future and then more quickly back into the past, is its path: a) ellipsoid; b) circular; c) N-shaped; or d) sigmoid?"

"Oh, I know this!" I shouted excitedly. "My aunt has a cyclotron in her kitchen, we used to play with it all the time! It's c) N-shaped!"

"Do you want more time with this? You're absolutely sure?"

"I am, Tania."

"So that's your final answer?"

"By golly, it is."

There was a long, suspenseful pause as Tania, who had as much under-standing of the question she'd asked me as she did of how dust bunnies are made, waited for the correct response to appear on the screen in front of her. Finally it did.

"You have just won a temporary waiver application!" she screamed tri-umphantly. Applause erupted, balloons wafted to the ceiling, and bouncy music blared.

I was, and am, of course, incredibly proud. I got great national exposure and I'm working this very day in staff development while I work toward my official certification in two years. This is truly a great country. And maybe before I get my certification I can get on the show again—and have the chance to win yet another nonrenewable temporary waiver! A guy can dream, can't he?

Singin' the Blues
for a Real Good Cause

It was dusk on the delta. As I headed home from school, I gazed upon the confluence of the mighty 101 and the turgid 280, the great rivers glistening sultry in the orange evening air. I could hear the Mercedes and Lexi as a flock of venture capitalists passed by. Somewhere in the distance I heard, too, the mournful wail of CEOs desperately trying to coax just a few more millions from their investment firms. I could also hear—if I listened hard—the crushed hopes, the lost dreams, the cruel lash of fate in a world that doesn't care how people make their preternatural fortunes. It was almost palpable at this time of day, when the engineers, the executives, the entrepreneurs, the VCs—the denizens of the great Silicon Delta—all finally leave their crowded cubicles, if only for a few brief hours.

This was the community into which I was sent to forge new alliances with my school, in the daring effort to make a difference! I was almost overwhelmed with the sheer weight of this backwater world. But I knew the future of our school rested with daring ventures such as this. Where to begin?—I asked myself.

I needed a break—a rest to gather my scattered senses and to contemplate anew the challenge before me. Up ahead I saw a sign for a Stardust Coffee Shop. It was a beckoning oasis and I pulled into the parking lot. How could I have known that the synchronicity about to unfold inside would change the fortunes of my school forever? Well? I'm waiting … Okay, if you don't know, I'll just go on.

I walked into the Stardust and was immediately assaulted by signs in nine languages offering 183 different kinds of coffee. I had to consult my periodic table of caffeine to make a selection and shortly received a cup containing a liquid not unlike the silt one sees so commonly on the delta. To this day I'm still uncertain whether it was my first sip that caused my hair to stand on end and my nails to instantly grow a half inch, or if it was the music I suddenly heard behind me.

I'd never heard anything like it. The sorrowful sounds arising in melodic cries from the two musicians perched in a dim corner of the Stardust seemed to capture the direst suffering and hurt of the Silicon Delta. What music it was! To the untrained ear, it was almost embarrassingly simple, disguising its underlying lack of complexity. It was sung without regard to sophistication or finesse, a style I learned later the performers chose carefully to best showcase their musical capabilities. They were unconcerned with such uppity fine points as listenability, intonation, or precision; their sole aim was to give voice to the turmoil of, as they put it, earning the lottery in Silicon Valley.

They were known only by their noms d'angst: "Doc" Bluetooth O'Toole and Nearsighted Java Bean. They were, I was to learn, the premier bluesmen of the Silicon Delta. Their hard times had become almost legendary; each once had to take a salary as low as the high $50s. Each had, at one point, been forced to drive an American car. And each of these hapless souls had been seen on meridians holding an ink jet-printed sign with a plaintive, heart-wrenching message: "Will write code for stock options." Now, I discovered, their voices were legendary throughout several square

miles. I listened in astonished admiration as the duo performed all their greatest hits, including "You're a Code Crackin' Mama But I Like You," "Got a Meetin' in the Mornin' and I Don't Care," and "Silicon Gone."

But the true epiphany for me occurred when I approached them after their concert as they were packing up their guitars and all the loose sugar they could find.

"You guys were incredible," I said.

"Yes," Bean answered laconically.

O'Toole glanced around the room wistfully. "Almost reminds me of my education days," he said.

I was thunderstruck. "What?! You were an educator?"

"Sure, kid," O'Toole said. "I once played all the top institutions. I don't miss the paperwork, but I sure miss the kids."

"What happened?"

"I succumbed to the lure of the Delta, the sirens of success and wealth. Once you get a taste for instant millions, don't kid yourself, it's hard to go back. But fate is a fickle mistress, as we sing in our hit "Fission Chips," and before I knew it I was in a vicious cycle of expansion and divestiture. If only there were a way I could contribute once more to education ... "

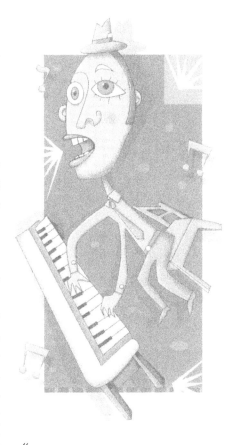

My mind was spinning. "I believe there is such a way," I said. The two bluesmen turned to me expectantly. I put to them a plan that dazzled me even as the ideas entered my head. "Why don't you do a string of benefit concerts for schools, right here in the Delta, targeting all the wealthy denizens still longing, like you, for a way to make a difference? We can call it Ed Aid."

The eyes of the great bluesmen lit up.

"When do we start?" Bean asked.

And that's how the Ed Aid concerts that you've heard so much about got started. The PBS special airs next month, and there's already talk of a movie featuring O'Toole and Bean, with other Delta blues luminaries such as Idaho Fillups, Startup Stu Twoshoes and Delta Don. There's an online site with sound clips of O'Toole and Bean and a link to make online donations. The only difficulty now seems to be that the bluesmen may be getting too happy to sing the blues, though it's anticipated that having them review a typical school budget will probably bring them back down.

A Clearer Seer: The Education Prophecies of NostraCosa
Desire you to know the future of education?

As we consider our visions of the future of education, it strikes me as most appropriate to revisit the prophetic literature of perhaps the greatest writer of educational divination. I speak, of course, of the masterful 16th-century prophet and poet, Nostracosa. Sadly overshadowed by his more renowned contemporary, Nostradamus, Nostracosa even today must battle skeptics who disparagingly take him for a wanton rip-off, a seer sucker, an untalented prophet wannabe. As we shall see, these vicious attacks are intermittently unwarranted.

Nostracosa wrote in quatrains, usually high-speed ones that ran a busy commuter schedule between Bologna and Islip, and curiously the name also of the poetic form he used. The literary quatrain was a simple four-line stanza of poetry Nostracosa used to obliquely describe in free-verse poetry his striking visions of the future, often seeing centuries beyond his own time. He is perhaps best known, to the degree that he is at all, for his prophecy of the 1969 New York Mets winning the World Series, in this quatrain celebrated in sports bars throughout the country:

"They that swing mighty sticks named for nocturnal flying rodents
Shall rise from east of the East River
In scant years of their origin
They shall take the series of the world"
(We are, of course, using the Fournier translations of the Nostracosa literature, considered by many to be the best guesses at the sometimes painfully obscure nuances of the prophet's writings.)

In 1547, Nostracosa anticipated the current craze of 900-number psychics when he began the world's first pay-for-service astrological readings. In my far-ranging research, I have uncovered the first known extant copy of an advertisement Nostracosa placed in his local paper, the *Renaissance Enquirer*. The translation reads as follows:

"Desire you to be cognizant of your financial fortunes? Wish you to know the mysterious workings of your way in this world? How's your love life? I hold the answers to these and other questions. Write today for your free introductory reading, and other readings will come automatically to you each month for a most reasonable fee. For a slightly higher fee, these readings can be stopped."

Clearly Nostracosa was a sharp cookie. This is further evident in his fabled foretelling of the development of Silicon Valley and its attendant technological revolution, in Quatrain 551, Track 19: "Hey how about those techies?

Near a city by the Bay, the other city, without the cable cars,
Powerful machines made in the valley of the silly cones
Shall transform the meaning of calculating"

But Nostracosa was concerned with much more than sports and silicon; his focus was primarily on education and technology, though some have argued without merit, in my view, that the differentiations among these topics are too slight to separate.

It was, after all, Nostracosa who predicted the rise of the Frederick Taylor model of education in the United States in the early 20th century, in this profound quatrain:

"In that land named after an Italian cartographer (why?),
A mere 500 years hence
Shall a Taylor tailor-make learning
Tailored to take the toiling trades as highest"

The almost whimsical alliteration was perhaps Nostracosa's way of softening the impact of what he prophesied. Nostracosa often employed such devices to mollify the blow of foreseen terrors. Take, for example, his pained constraint as he depicted the misguided rise of standardized testing:

"They shall measure not the true minds of learners,
Preferring to prepare them only for mindless jobs

In which these now intellectually destitute shall inquire of their patrons: 'Do you desire fries to accompany that order?'"

But let us turn now to Nostracosa's prophecies in the field of education technology that have yet to be fulfilled. Let's see what we have to look forward to—or perhaps to dread, and thus forewarned, find a way to leave town. Let's take a look first at a most unique way Nostracosa sees that learning will occur in the century now unfolding before us:

"In schools near the year 2001 shall students
Inhale their learning, quite literally,
For lessons shall be contained in nasal spray
And be time-released into young minds all the day"

Sounds too fantastic? Remember, that's what they said about the famed Nostracosa prediction of a crashless version of Windows; only time will have the final say.

In this well-known quatrain, Nostracosa teases us with an enticing vision of the schools of the future:

"Within vast mercantile centers called malls
Near such merchants as Mont … [indecipherable] Wards
Shall tiny booths be built at which students may stop by
And grab a quick bite and their academic assignments"

Nostracosa gives us a sense of a remarkable new resource teachers will use to facilitate their teaching in this quatrain:

"There will be made a machine that can tap into
The limitless knowledge of all things that all teenagers know they possess
The machine will transfer this omniscience
Into classroom curricula"

As for pedagogy, Nostracosa foresees a time when a project-based, multiple-intelligences approach to education will be the norm. He predicts a time when learning will be based on use of every aspect of the mind and learning styles, and when assessment is based on discernment of acquired learning through carefully planned projects:

"They shall study motion, music and mathematics
Through performing that ritual that shall be called the Hokey Pokey:
What is put in shall be likewise put out
And measured in new variations"

Of course the future does not progress without some obstacles. Nostracosa warns of the dangers to education of politicking, which we saw no small amount of during the campaign of the last year. Once again eerily accurate, Nostracosa saw, half a millennium ago, who would win the last presidential election and why:

"He shall assume the office that is oval
Who promises reform and betterment for schools and learning,
Has hair and wears no glasses,
And whose last name has only four letters"

Some argue, as some are wont to do, that this prediction could have gone either way. Let the Philistines quibble if they must. To we who understand, this quatrain is astonishingly on target.

All in all, it's a bold and bright new future out there for education. Can it truly be that a sage from five centuries ago foretold it all? The proof is indisputable. It remains only for us to listen, learn and make our way along the unfolding path before us, so brightly illuminated by the forgotten prophet, Nostracosa.

The Blazing Electrons'
Winning Season

E-learning, as you may have learned if you live above ground and within sight of a computer, is the new hot thing in education. How big has it gotten and how helpful is it, really? I'm glad you asked, particularly since this chapter is going to be on this very topic.

The largest university system in the United States today is the mighty E. U., with campuses located… well, pretty much every place that has electricity. There should be nothing read into the fact that most people pronounce the name of this huge institution "Eeeeeyuu."

How has the excitement over e-learning changed college life these days? Let's take a closer look. Did you know that E. U. has sports teams? Sure it does; what's a college without a team to root for? The E. U. football team is called the Blazing Electrons. Here's the team cheer:

"Fight on, brave Electrons, flow swiftly to the end!
Match the speed of light, cause space-time to bend!
Push 'em back, push 'em back, waaaaay back!
Circle that nucleus and go on the attack!"

Pretty stirring stuff, huh? When the team has a winning season, its listserv can contain several hundred thousand email addresses. Try getting that many people into a typical college sports stadium!

E-learning is important also because it's preparing students for a society that will run totally online. Classrooms across America are getting kids ready for the world that arrives tomorrow. An early indication of what that world may look like is shown in the fact that this year, for the very first time, the Teacher of the Year Award goes to a very nice laptop computer at E. U. Okay, I'm making this up, but let's pretend I'm serious. Here's how a recent interview I had with the new Teacher of the Year went:

"So, Mr. E. U. Computer, you must be very proud," I began.

"You bet," the computer typed back at me. "We machines have made giant strides in human history lately. This is a major reaffirmation of our worth."

"Are the rumors of you and the Internet getting into a very serious relationship at all true?"

"You know, the Internet and I are really just very good friends. We're very close, but I take exception to that picture that recently ran in the tabloids showing us sharing circuitry."

"Of course. Didn't mean to touch a nerve. So do you have a lot of students scanning in a picture of an apple and sending it to you?"

"No, these days if you want to be a real teacher's pet, you don't need fruit. You need added memory. It's like when God asked Abraham to prepare a sacrifice and Isaac asked him where they were going to get something to sacrifice, and Abraham answered, 'Don't worry, my son, God will supply the RAM.' "

"Computer humor, huh?"

"I got a million of 'em. Hey, how many programmers does it take to change a light bulb? None. That's a hardware problem."

"So, as an online teacher, what advantages do you believe you have over other teachers?"

"Well, the big thing, of course, is that I can take a student almost anywhere in the world, electronically speaking. Soon there will be more Web pages on the Net than there are people in the world. I can instantly access the gazillions, not to get too technical here, of educational resources available on the Web."

"Why don't you give us a few examples? Let's say, for instance, that we want to do a project on microbiology."

"Coming right up." The Teacher of the Year whirred briskly for a few seconds, then stopped. "I have a whole bunch of URLs for you. Shall we visit some and see what we've got?"

"Sure."

"Okay. First stop: invisiblethings.com. Oh, this looks really good. Here's what it says: 'The Internet's premiere location for the serious student of the unseeable.' "

"Sounds promising. So that's a good first place to start?"

"Well, wait a minute. I'm reading further down. It says, 'Yes, if you're looking for advice from beyond on life, love, and work, sign on now for your reading! Only $4.99 per question, billed directly to your credit card!' "

"Well, goodness knows, doing a search on something as broad as microbiology could easily produce hits that might miss the target. Why don't we try something else? How about, say, U.S. presidential elections?"

"Good one. Here we go. First hit: take me to your leader.com. Let's check it out. Hmm, looks promising. It starts, 'The home of the Web's best research on the electoral process.' "

"Ah. Real academic content."

"Let's see what else it's got. It goes on, 'We've scoured the world for the best sightings of UFOs, and now it's your turn to vote for the top 10!' "

"I suppose this could be pertinent if we believe what the tabloids have said about presidential candidates meeting with aliens. Like the one that had that photo of Clinton shaking hands with that creature from *Close Encounters*."

"Well, there you go. Not only can the Web give you an incredible array of educational resources, but it also affords the student vast creativity in determining how to make it relevant to the topic at hand. What more could you ask for?"

"Might this also suggest that perhaps technology needs input and guidance from a human source? Perhaps careful selectivity in ensuring that Web hits actually are appropriate and useful?"

"Hey, I see no reason why humans and machines can't work side by side in complete harmony, for common cause and betterment. This isn't Planet of the Computers, you know."

"That's probably part of the graciousness that got you elected Teacher of the Year."

"I like to think so."

"Do you think a computer will take the prestigious honor of Teacher of the Year again in years to come?"

"Well, I'm no psychic. I read the future only according to my programming. But I don't see why not. We're cute, friendly, and very fast. I'm not saying every teacher should have to meet those criteria, but let's face it, it doesn't hurt."

"So how else is e-learning improving the human condition?"

"Well, here at E. U., we're very excited about the Blazing Electrons, of course."

"I love their cheer."

"They're 8 and 2 this year, against some very tough opponents. The really big game is this Saturday, when they play their archrivals, the Computer University Slippery Quarks. They're a very tough team; you just never really know where they are."

"Not to mention the fact that they can be either particles or waves."

"And then there's the whole thing with the observer affecting them just by observing them. I mean, what does that do when the officials take a look at their play? I think the university sports association is going to take a close look at the rule book this year to see if they can really do those things."

"Be sure to have them pass that on to the scientific community. I'm sure they'd be keenly interested in the ruling."

"It's just another way e-learning is helping, even through sports."

To Spin, Perchance to Dream

I work in that fabled town they call the Dream Factory, where creative geniuses work their magic to create the grand illusions that entertain the nation and the world, where fantasy is spun into the fabric of our daily lives, where familiar faces that grace our screens live, work and play. Washington, DC.

I'm one of those creative geniuses, one of the best and don't you forget it because if you do, I'm out of a job. Yeah, I'm a spinmeister, a master of reframing with a Ph.D. in power lunches. I can make you think green is yellow, yesterday is tomorrow and not inhaling is the same as never smoking.

I've worked a lot of campaigns, and I was getting kind of bored, if you want to know the truth. I'd just wrapped up an incredible masterpiece, a work so outrageous even I couldn't quite believe it, having to do with selling a certain alcoholic beverage using talking reptiles and amphibians. I was definitely ready to move on. So I was intrigued when I got the call from the school.

"We need help," they said.

"Can you afford me?" I asked, cutting right to the chase.

"Well, we think we can hire you under the provisions of a grant we got for developing a creative writing course."

"I'm there."

Next day I'm sitting in a room full of educator-types. Boy, could I do an image makeover on these guys. "What do you need?" I asked.

"Money," one of them said.

I reached for my cell phone and my Altoids. "Gentlemen, I'm outta here. You led me to believe you could pay for me."

"And we can," he responded. I sat back down. "But all schools need a constant flow of money. We're always writing new grant proposals."

"So?"

"So, we need new, creative proposals. Money sources are tired of the same-old same-old. We need someone to help us—what's the word?—reposition our requests. You know, dress them up, give them a fresh angle."

"Put a new spin on 'em," I said, getting the picture. "Reframe those puppies. Give 'em some razzle-dazzle, some sparkle, make 'em larger than life."

"Exactly."

"I can do this. Let's get to it. Give me something you need money for."

They pulled out a long list. "Well, okay," the head educator-type said.

"Let's start with this one. Our school needs an Excedrin/Advil bulk dispenser."

"Excuse me?"

"This is a school," he explained. "If the students don't need them, the teachers do."

I thought for a moment, which, yes, okay, if you're going to get picky, is far longer than it should've taken. But this was a new field for me. "Guys," I said, "you don't need an Excedrin/Advil bulk dispenser."

"But we just ..."

"What you need, and what you're going to demand from anyone who has both money and brains, is a Specialized User Retrieval Device to monitor enhancement effects of over-the-counter medicinal substances. Cost: $3,000+."

There were the expected ohs and ahs. "You're good," one educator said.

"I know. Next item."

"Our computers are all elderly," he continued. "They're older than our students, and many of them are wheezing with advanced emphysema. We'd like money for a whole new fleet of them, tied into a new T1 line and LAN."

"Wrong," I said. "The urgency is overwhelming, and what you want on your desk within the hour is funding for an Integrated Computational Overland Connectivity System, with Individuated Operational Units for Direct User-Interface Control Capability. A million five, easy. No self-respecting educational institution could be expected to operate without one."

"Gosh," someone in the room said, "can we get one of those, too?"

The head educator jumped in. He was clearly emboldened, his imagination catching fire from the winds of inspiration I was fanning on his frail spark. "Is there ...?" He struggled with the enormity of the idea overtaking him. "Is there anything we can't ask for? I mean, with the right reframing?"

"Guy," I said, beginning to take to the man. "May I call you 'guy'? Take your best shot."

He glanced around the room, looking for signs of support. "Go ahead, Ed," the man at his side assured him. "I wouldn't have dared," Ed started. "But, well, the average temperature in our classrooms is the same as the average age of our teachers: 45. We were wondering about getting a new furnace."

"Wow. Give me a moment to recover." What I said in gentle sarcasm was taken seriously, as they respectfully paused. "Here's what we request, fellas. You want half a million for a new research facility to be contained in a specialized school chamber, carefully contained in the building's lower level. It's a Heat Generation Storage and Osmosification Device. And you need another half a mil for professional development for the device. I mean, I presume you're going to need a janitor, right?" I must admit I enjoyed the awe that swept the room. "How do you do it?" someone asked.

"People, you're looking at a man who once took a tax deduction on a fur coat for his wife by claiming it as insulation. What's next?"
A man in the back raised his hand. "I've got one."

Ed interrupted him immediately. "Oh, Ben, you're not going to talk about your silly science fiction project, are you?"

Ben was undeterred. "Do you suppose we could get funding for my work on transgenerational timeshifting?" he asked. A rush of embarrassment swept over the rest of the room. But not over me.

"Ben," I said, "where would any of us be if we didn't dare to dream the impossible? Do you think the Taco Bell people paused for a second before they launched a campaign to sell nachos with a Chihuahua uglier than sin? I think not. Consider the daring of Apple and their Think Different campaign; they ran it even though they knew every English teacher on the planet would come after them screaming, it's an adverb! How about the bold thinking that led some inspired bureaucrat to coin the obviously oxymoronic term government organization? I have no idea what you just asked for, but you go for it, Ben."

I worked that room well into the night. By the time we were finished, we had grant proposals for things ranging from park benches to time machines, though of course, you'd never recognize any of the requests by those names. Vertical Weight Distribution Devices. Nonlinear Experiential Waveshift Transformers. Finally I got up to leave, telling them I had to run out and do some urgent research. Then I left and caught a movie.

How Doc the Techie Saved Our School

I was talking with my tech coordinator the other day, who is also my chiropractor and my securities advisor. As my school's resident techie, he's pretty much the guy everyone goes to for most anything.

Just yesterday, I saw someone stop him in the hall and ask him, "So, Doc," as he is affectionately known because he's also a doctor, "how much of a firewall do you think we need?"

"Well," Doc answered, "depends on whether we go with a T1 or a DSL."

Right after that, someone else came up to him and said, "Doc, I can't get my coffee mug to fit into the cup holder on my computer. What's wrong? And can you recommend a safe retirement investment?"

"It's not a cup holder," Doc said. "It's a CD drive. Go with long-term mutual funds that invest in online education."

Doc the Techie is just one of those geniuses who goes through life with straight A's in everything. He's the guy who turned one of the most amazing new ventures into a multimillion-dollar IPO. You've heard of it: Homeless.com. Yeah, that's right, Doc's the man who got a bunch of homeless people together, helped

them create their own Web site, leveraged it into a portal page with 12 million hits a day, generated banner ads from the likes of Cistern Systems (their tag line: "They may not have a home, but they've got a home page—thanks to us") and Okidoki Enterprises ("We're not just all right—we're Okidoki"). Soon the homeless were being called the Million-Dollar Nomads, wearing thousand-dollar suits and partying out of gigantic Winnebagos, rapidly becoming the nouveau riche of the Silicon Valley.

As Doc was adjusting my sacroiliac the other day, I took the opportunity to question him about a problem that was nagging me almost as much as my back. "Doc," I said, "our school needs to raise a bunch of money, and for some reason they've asked me to head that effort, even though I once tried to do a tax deduction on a fur coat as home insulation. What should I do?"

"Hold on a sec," Doc said, picking up a sheet of music manuscript paper. "Just need to finish the last two bars of my piano concerto and I'm all yours." He scrawled some meaningful sixteenth notes for the contrabassoon and finally turned to me again.

"Okay, money for the school," he said. "I tell you what we do: You call a meeting of key school personnel, and I'll help brainstorm some cool marketing ideas."

"Thanks, Doc. You're a lifesaver."

"I know."

A week later the school cafeteria/server station was crowded with school people ready to market till they dropped. Doc kicked things off. "All right," he said, "why don't we just free-associate some ideas for marketing slogans for the school?"

Mrs. Weemsley, the etiquette and psychogenic sciences teacher, volunteered, "How about: 'Our school—it's not so bad'?"

"Okay, anyone else?" Doc said. "Now, let's not always see the same hands."

Biff Connoly, drama coach and advanced apathy instructor, said, "Well, I don't really care one way or another, but if I had to make a big entrance, I might say something like, 'Our school—take it or leave it.' "

"Hmm," Doc said diplomatically. "Let's give that some thought. Or not. Anyone else?"

Stomp Hoffer, apparent paradoxes and time travel teacher, suddenly said, "I've just arrived from the last two minutes and I am here to speak to you from the past. Sorry I'm late. How about, 'Our school—hey, your kids have to go somewhere'?"

"We'll get back to you on that, Stomp," Doc said gracefully.

"I have a thought," said Barker Sideman, our instructor of quixotic economics. "Maybe we could file an antitrust suit against ourselves, the whole education field, for being a monopoly. You know, like when the government filed suit against Macrosoft. Maybe the publicity would drive in more interest and money, the way it did for Macrosoft."

"That's creative, Barker," Doc said, "but we need to ramp up faster."

Then he lowered his head and went into a sudden reverie of contemplation. All in the room knew that he was in that most special place in the mind where genius goes to gather its metaphoric kindling and gently fan the sparks of rumination that would ultimately billow into majestic flames of profundity and luminosity.

"Would you look at that," Doc finally said. "I've got a spaghetti stain on my tie."

That was Doc for you, always lightening a mood. But then, he swung around and rose dramatically to his feet. "I've got it!" he cried. "We'll do a Well-Adjusted Wired Kids campaign!"

I think I spoke for the rest of us when I said, "Huh?"

"Don't you see? Here's how we pitch it: We're not just about getting your kids wired and online. Sure, we're that; we're always on the cutting edge of classroom technology. But we're also concerned about your kids being well-adjusted. That's why at our school, we also do chiropractic adjustments, to make sure our students are both techno-hip and subluxation-free! I'll do adjustments on our kids and donate the fees back to the school!"

We were, of course, stunned, dazzled yet again at Doc's uncanny brilliance. The Well-Adjusted Wired Kids campaign was one of Doc's best ideas, and we and our students were to be its direct beneficiary. But he wasn't finished.

"Tell you what else I'll do," he said. "As you know, my last three books have all been bestsellers. The last one, *Polyphasia for Fun and Profit*, is being made into a movie starring that cute dog on *Frasier*. What no one knows yet is that I have a new book coming out this summer."

That Doc! Just when you thought he couldn't surprise you more!

"And I'm going to give all the profits from the book to the school," he said with a dramatic flourish.

Once again, we were speechless. Finally, I asked him, "What's this book, Doc?"

"It's called *Our Fighting Men in Uniform: A Guide to Hockey.*"

Well, the rest of the story is well-known. The Well-Adjusted Wired Kids campaign went on to make gazillions of dollars, give or take a few. The dog from *Frasier* turned in an astonishing performance in *Polyphasia* and made us all proud. The hockey book became a World Wrestling Federation TV special and went through the roof, with proceeds from that enhancing the school's coffers as well.

All I can say is, thank goodness we have a school system that can attract people like Doc to become tech coordinators!

Totally Unrehearsed Techno Telemarketing
The Perfect Answer for School Technology Needs

I was working late into the evening in my classroom the other day when I heard the school phone ring. Silly me, I answered it.

"Hello [insert name here]. This is Bob at Such a Steal Enterprises, and I'm calling this evening with news about incredible deals on products you can't possibly go on living another minute without. Have I caught you at a good time, [insert name here]?"

"No," I said with what I thought to be a particularly convincing tone.

"That's great, [insert name here]. Now, I want you to know that I'm not reading from a script turn page here." I heard the sound of paper turning. Then he went on: "Insert name here, I'm speaking straight from the heart here. Now, [insert name here], I'll bet you've been thinking a lot lately about the new technology your school needs, right?"

I thought I'd throw him a curve, just to see if I could derail his train of thought—if there was one. "Actually," I said, "I was just reflecting on the fact that those who forget the pasta are condemned to reheat it."

"But you've been wondering just what kind of new technology you need," he rolled on undeterred. "That's why this evening, I'm your very best friend."

"Your pants are on fire," I said, to keep myself entertained.

"And well you might ask," he went on. "Well, first let's talk about this little technological gem no school can be without. We call it (pause for emphasis) the Textbook Humidifier!"

I was kind of sad to actually get engaged in the conversation, but I said: "What?"

"Yes, [insert name here], you heard me right—the Textbook Humidifier! Say, how many times have you stood before a classroom with a textbook in your hand with writing so dry you could plant a cactus?"

"What does the script you're not reading from say I'm supposed to say here?" I inquired.

"Exactly," Bob continued. "The Textbook Humidifier is the perfect answer to all that snooze-inducing text in the classroom."

"How does it work?"

"You're probably wondering how it (turn page here) works. Speak simply as if talking to a child remember these are teachers you just take any textbook in your classroom and place it in the Humidifier. Choose a humidifying setting: Drenched for those unbelievably dry texts, Just Saturated for your average text, or Lightly Moistened for that rare book that's intermittently interesting. Hit the button and (enthusiastically) poof! there you are, text wet enough to put out a fire. Have you ever heard of anything like this, [insert name here; pause for response] ?"

"I hate to say this, but that actually sounds useful. Does it work on Web and computer-based stuff, too?"

"I thought not. But it gets better, [insert name here; speak in friendlier tone]. It also works on Web and computer-based stuff, too. You can place an entire computer in the Humidifier and get rid of dry language on every Web site and every computer document you encounter. Pretty amazing, isn't it (answer for him/her)? Sure it is. You're probably thinking I put this little speech of mine through a Humidifier, right (chuckle pleasantly)?"

"Oh, absolutely," I said. "You are definitely all wet."

"Now, insert name here, how much would you pay for a technology tool like this?"

"$1.98."

"Four thousand dollars? Five thousand (pause, and let the figures sink in) these people aren't rocket scientists?"

"Actually, I teach rocket science. But don't let me throw you off track."

"Well, [insert name here], if you order today, this amazing little gem is yours for the unbelievably low price of (dramatic pause) $3,995! What, you say, how can we afford to just give this stuff away? Why don't we just rip the shirts right off our backs and hand them to you (laugh good-naturedly)? Well, it's because of nice folks like you try not to gag when you read this line who keep buying in such volume that allows us to keep our prices low, low, low!"

"I'm so glad I could help."

"Now, [insert name here], (it's time to keep this drivel moving there's another dozen calls to make), let's get down to nuts and bolts."

"Sure. I used to teach shop."

"Are you the person at your school authorized to make purchases assume he is because we don't care who signs for it as long as somebody's on record as having ordered?"

"I'm allowed to buy candy out of the machine."

"That's great, [insert name here, keep it rolling before he has time to reconsider]. Now, the Text Humidifier comes in a choice of three lovely colors. Would you like brown, black or white (don't bother waiting for the answer most people won't send it back anyway)?"

"Do you have it in mauve?"

"Fine, white it is. So that's one Text Humidifier in white for $3,995, plus a very low shipping and handling charge (absolutely do not break out laughing at this). Now, before I go, [insert name here], I just want to let you know of one little bonus item that I'm authorized to offer you only at this particular time (keep a straight face again). Did you know that calculator holsters are all the rage these days? Of course you did. All the Silicon Valley engineers are wearing them these days, and we all know what fashion trendsetters they are. They're what everyone is calling tech-no cool (make him feel like an idiot if he doesn't know the term). I'm authorized to include four calculator holsters in this order for you, at the incredibly low price of $24.95 per holster. You're right, the price is insane. And you get them for only a very slight increase in your shipping and handling charges (yeah like 200 percent)."

"I suppose I should be impressed that you're actually able to read this script you're not reading from."

"All I need from you for a go-ahead on this order is any motion in any direction of your head or any other body part."

"So to turn this order down, basically I'd have to drop dead?"

"Fine, we'll process this and get your order out to you this very day."

"I can't tell you how that makes me feel."

"Now, don't try to tell me how that makes you feel. (Get all gooey and emotional here) you know, [insert name here], we at Such a Steal Enterprises take such pride in our work. Just knowing we're out there, doing our part to make your life easier, making a difference in your day, changing lives one by one (pause and sob gently speak very quietly) well, it (just turn page now) makes us feel so darned good."

"(Pause and look pleadingly at the clock) Bob, I know you've got to get to those other dozen calls."

"In fact, [insert name here], you know what I'm going to do make it sound like this just occurred to you? I'm going to waive the sales tax on this sale (don't give him time to point out that there's not supposed to be sales tax on it anyway)."

"I feel so special."

"No, I insist. Here at Such a Steal, it's not about the money (keep that face straight). Thank you for your time (now get him off the line), and have a wonderful day (return to start of script for next call)."

Suddenly he was gone. A student came in and asked for me, but I didn't recognize my name. "Sorry," I told him. "I only answer to 'insert name here.'"

Here's the Windup and the Pitch!

I guess I'll never forget Professor Smith—no, it was Jones. I probably learned more about entrepreneurial enterprise in higher education from him than anyone else, except possibly from state lotteries. He commanded respect by his very presence. I remember that first day in marketing class. "Listen up, people," he began, "the person with a degree in engineering asks, 'How can this be built?' The person with a degree in accounting asks, 'How much will this cost?' And the person with a degree in liberal arts asks, 'Do you want fries with that?' What does this teach us? Anyone? And let's not always see the same hands."

There was a momentary stirring among us. I felt the answer creeping into my consciousness, but feeling chastened for my audacity in this rarefied atmosphere, I did not move. The professor sensed this in me, I believe, or else noticed me starting to nod off. He picked me out of the crowd.

"You," he said.

I paused for composure, then responded. "Well, I suppose it explains why so many liberal arts majors go into professional sports."

"Yes," he agreed, "and also why you hear stories like Shaquille O'Neal being asked if he visited the Parthenon while he was in Greece and answering, 'Well, I can't really remember the names of the clubs we went to.' But not all of us can expect to become sports superstars. And if we wish to bring in a more substantial bottomline to our colleges, we have to think bigger."

"Excuse me," I interjected. "Do I understand you to say that a college can become a big moneymaker?"

"You bet, so to speak," he responded. "Higher education is among America's top international exports, right up there with entertainment and arms." (This, by the way, turns out to be true.) "We need to start marketing higher education the way the big boys do."

"What are you saying?" I queried.

"I'm talking professional endorsements for higher ed."

A murmur of astonishment swept through the room as we struggled to get our minds around the magnitude of this thought.

"Work with me here, people," he went on. "I want you to do more than just imagine this. I've brought in some major talent to help me demonstrate. Gentlemen, please come in." Through the classroom door entered a small group of men, all of them instantly recognizable to anyone familiar with their sports. We were stunned. Professor Jones (or was it Smith?) had managed to assemble world-renowned athletes to join his marketing class. "Please give us some examples of big-name endorsements for higher ed," he said to the group.

A lanky young man with a golfing cap stepped forward first. "Hi," he said to an imaginary TV camera, "I'm Tiger Woods. You know, with a name like mine, I'm asked all the time, 'Hey, Tiger, you must really enjoy zoology.' Or 'Hey, Mr. Woods, where do you stand on the issue of rain

forest destruction?' Well, truth is, kids, I wouldn't have had a clue how to respond to these questions if it weren't for the fine folks down at State U. Yes, after a hard day of pounding the bejeebers out of a little white ball, I find there's nothing quite so intellectually stimulating as a few classes at the ol' university. Hey, take it from your pal, Tiger Woods: Get down to State U and take a double major!"

"That was terrific, Tiger," said Professor Whatshisname. "Next."

Up stepped Barry Bonds, the new all-time home-run hero. "Hey, kids," he said. "Quick: What's 73 minus 70? Sure, I threw you a curve here, a high, inside fastball. But you've got to be on your game if you're going to handle a question like that, which I got asked all the time after I hit 73 home runs. I had to know the difference between my 73 and Mark McGuire's previous record of 70. If you're getting out of high school like most kids these days, this could be a stumper for you. That's why you want to get on over to State U and learn yourself some higher math. Then you'll be hitting a home run every time you step up to the home plate of life."

"Great stuff, there, Barry," the professor said. "Next, let's hear from former football great and current ESPN sportscaster, Joe Theisman."

"Hi, kids," Joe said. "You know, I'll never forget that broadcast of mine when I told millions of viewers, 'Nobody in football should be called a genius. A genius is a guy like Norman Einstein.' Boy, was I right! Well, I was wrong, too, of course, but that's why I was right. Anyway, we in football aren't always noted for our logic. For example, I remember a college football coach who once told his team, 'You guys line up alphabetically by height.' Another time he said to them, 'Everybody pair up in groups of three.' And then there's the football senior who told the press, 'I'm going to graduate on time, no matter how long it takes.' Sure, we often don't know logic from logjam, which is just what happens to our brains sometimes. But I did something about it. I went back to State U for a refreshing course in remedial thinking. Now I can stand proud. Now I'm capable of correcting players when they say things like, 'My sister's expecting a baby, and I don't know if I'm going to be an uncle or an aunt.' Yes, kids, you, too, can think in nonself-contradictory statements. Pick up the phone and enroll today at State U. If you call right now, we'll include this lovely set of coasters with the school emblem absolutely free!"

"That's just a sampling," the professor said. "Think on these things. Class dismissed."

That night I dreamed. I saw the college reaping the benefits of major endorsements. I saw State U with franchises in every state and 14 foreign countries. I saw it rolling out a new line of sports watches. I saw it buying infomercials. I was overcome with entrepreneurial ecstasy. This, I realized, is the stuff dreams are made of, sometimes also with a side of pepperoni pizza.

How to Win the Assessment Game and a Nice Toaster

It was assessment time again and I was in my usual accountability stupor—eyes glazing over at the prospect of effectively gauging academic progress and efficacy. What I really need, I thought, was a knock at my door—someone selling some hot new products to make assessment incredibly easy.

Suddenly, there was a knock at the door.

I opened it. A gangly youth stood in the hall with a wild insouciance burning in his eyes that seemed to say, "Je ne sais quoi."

"Hi," he said with undisguised nonchalance. "I'm selling some hot new products to make assessment incredibly easy."

"You're kidding," I said.

"Not that I know of," he answered. "I have a pretty cool line of assessment tools that no self-respecting educator should be without. Allow me." He pushed his way into my office and within minutes had spread a dizzying array of high-tech bric-a-brac across the wilds of my desk.

"Let's start with something simple," my super salesman said. He held up something that looked a lot like those little eight balls that kids play with to ask questions and get random answers.

"It's a modified eight ball," the youth said, "like the ones kids play with. We've spruced up the answers to specifically address assessment questions. Go ahead, give it a spin." He handed me the device.

What the heck, I thought. "Okay. Will the bottom percentile of my class make it to grade level by next semester?" I turned the eight ball over and watched an answer float to the surface of the window on the bottom.

"Sources say count on it," the message informed me with an almost belligerent confidence. I wished I had its sources.

"What else you got?" I asked.

"Well, here's something hot off the assembly line. We can't keep 'em in stock." He pulled out a circular board and hung it on the wall of my office. It had concentric circles with writing in each circle.

"How do you use it?" I said. The kid handed me some darts.

"We call this approach 'induced synchronicity,'" he said. "You throw a dart, you see where it lands. The secret to its accuracy is that you have to take it seriously."

"I figured there had to be a catch." I decided to test it against results I'd spent hours arriving at the night before. With the scores of a particular situation in mind, I hurled a dart at the board. It thudded into a circle that read, "Much improvement needed; don't rush this one." Except for punctuation, the message was identical to my results. The board's punctuation was better.

I was impressed. "Any other goodies, kid?" I said, now with anticipation.

"You bet," he answered. From his case he unfolded another circular device, larger, with a lot more writing on it, and set it on another wall.

"This is my favorite," he said. "We call it the Wheel of Assessment."

It was glorious. It was huge and covered most of the wall. Its surface was divided into pie slices with different assessment quantifications, ranging from "Get real" to "I'd like to thank all the little people." At its top was a pointer; when the wheel was spun, the pointer landed on an assessment quantifier.

"Let me plug this puppy in," the kid said, and he did. Instantly a ring of light bulbs around the edge of the wheel illuminated. Music came on from internal speakers.

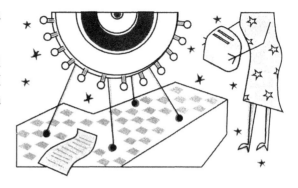

Balloons were released from the back of the wheel.

I was dazzled, but I had one concern. "But, kid," I said. "This'll never fly in education. It's too ... too "

"Las Vegas?"

"Well, yeah."

"Glad you brought that up. Here are the credentials of the creators." He handed me a sheet that listed the names of nine people who'd worked on the creation of the Wheel of Assessment. All had advanced degrees from the prestigious Fisher Price Foreign Institute of Technology in Upper Volta. "Hey, these people don't put their names on just anything, you know," the kid said reassuringly. "Want to give her a spin?"

I did, but something nagged at me. "There's something missing," I mused.

"Ah," he said. "I know what you need. You need the deluxe version. Just a second."

He bolted out the door and returned a moment later, with another man and a woman close behind him. As the couple entered my office, perky music suddenly exploded from somewhere, and an equally perky disembodied voice abruptly said, "Ladies and gentlemen and all you lucky educators, it's time to play—Wheel! Of! Assessment!"

The sound of a large audience applauding then arose from somewhere. The new man, dressed in a suit so shiny I could see my reflection, came to within a hair of my nose and started talking to me as if I were a distant camera. "Hey, welcome back to the show. Well, I guess you know how to play Wheel of Assessment, so let's get started. Wanda, get ready to spin!"

"I'm ready, Jack," the woman said. She was dressed in something that looked like it would make breathing dangerous, but she somehow floated to the wheel and draped an arm purposefully on it.

"Okay," Jack said, "let's find out what we're playing for. Who are we assessing first?" he asked me.

"Um" I began. "Well, you kind of caught me off guard here, but let's say I want to assess grade-level achievement in K-12 quantum experiential physics."

"All righty," Jack said, "though I might point out that the procedure for this is pretty much the same no matter what you're trying to assess. Wanda, give that thing a spin!"

Wanda did, and I can't express how relieved I was to discover that the Wheel proclaimed "You're the tops!" I went on to win a toaster and an all expense-paid trip to Bimidji, Minnesota, before the demo was completed. I also won the home assessment version of the game so I could apply this same advanced technology from the comfort of my own living room.

From Here to Perplexity

I'm Mr. Davis, professional staff development drill instructor. I take frazzled, terrified teachers and turn them into elite computer pros. It's like herding cats, and it's a dirty job, but somebody's got to do it.

"Listen up, troops," I shouted to the milling recruits. "From this moment on, your skinny backsides belong to me! I am no longer Mr. Davis, the teacher you know and love. From now on, I am the god of computers and all things pertaining thereto!"

"Wow," said one real space cadet. "So, do you have like a certificate that says that?"

I was on him like a grammar teacher on a misplaced modifier. "What was that, soldier?" I thundered.

"Uh, excuse me," said a nerdy type next to him. "I believe what the gentleman was endeavoring to inquire was, albeit in perhaps a jocular manner, whether or not there is a certification process to establish your credentials as the deity in whose charge all things related to com ..."

"Soldier, was I talking to you?" I demanded.

"Uh, no, quite so, I see your point," he replied.

"Hit the floor and give me 20," I shouted.

The nerd looked very confused. He shrugged his shoulders, then bent down, struck the floor with his fist, got back up, took out his wallet, and pulled out a $20 bill. "I really don't see how this benefits our training ..."

"Let's try this again, troops," I said. "You're here to become crack computer pros. I'm the guy who's gonna get you there. You don't breathe, you don't move, you don't even think unless you do it through me during this training. You understand me, maggots?"

"Excuse me, Sarge," said a woman in the second row, with a not inconsiderable sarcasm. "I'm with HR. You can't call us 'maggots.' Not without thorough documentation." Each group gets harder and harder to deal with, I thought. I took a deep breath and started over. "Alright, troops. Anybody here ever had any computer or information services experience before?"

"Yeah, Sarge," said a guy in the back. "I was the technology guru at my school."

"You were?"

"Sure. Well, you know, among other things."

"Like what?"

"Well, I was also the custodian." I struggled to keep the confusion I felt from showing. "How's that, trooper?"

"Well. they didn't know where to put the new network server. So one day I came in and opened the supply closet, and there was the server. Plugged in right next to the sink. Wires coming in from the ceiling. It was cool."

"The server was in the supply closet?"

"Oh, yeah. Wasn't too bad, although it got a little harder to get my mops in the sink. And then, of course, I was trying to keep water from spilling on it, you know, that was something of a challenge." He suddenly grew very serious. "And I never got a drop on it," he continued. "I guess that's why they figured I had the right stuff." He paused, then sheepishly added, "And you know, that one big accident wasn't really my fault."

"Accident?"

"Well, yeah. See, one morning everybody came in and found the network was on, but nobody could access anything."

"And why was that?"

He grew teary. "It wasn't my fault. See, they didn't plan it right."

"What happened, soldier?"

"Well, nobody told me it would take hours to restart the whole network. I needed to run the floor polisher. There wasn't another plug around there. So I ... I ..."

"You unplugged the server to run the floor polisher?"

"Well, I plugged it back in again when I was finished. It wasn't my fault! I mean, they just went to Circuit City or somewhere and came back with a new toy and didn't know where to plug it in."

I let loose a sigh. "Alright, recruits. Break in place. Smoke 'em if you got 'em." I took a moment to consider my next approach. After a few minutes I called the group back to attention. "Now, you mag ... er, recruits. Let's go through your familiarization drill. Now. You're in your classroom. You're running your computer. Suddenly it freezes up. You stand there in front of the whole class, who is watching you with an evil glee. Beads of sweat start to run down your face. You stammer. You stall. Then a 14-year-old kid in the front offers to fix it for you. What do you do?"

"Sarge," one recruit said, "are we on a Mac or a PC?"

"Does it make a difference to you, soldier?" I queried.

"Well, sure. See, then we could say to the kid, 'Well, I'd like to let you help, but this is a Mac.' Or a PC. Whichever is the opposite of what the kid says he can handle."

"You're not thinking, soldier. Kids today are ambiplatform." A sullen dismay swept onto the recruit's face.

"I got it, Sarge," said another trooper. "We say, 'Can't let you help. It'd void the warranty.'"

"And then what?"

"Then I walk down the hall and leave a note for the MIS guy on the supply room door."

The MIS janitor spoke up. "See, that's good. That way, you know, right after I move some

tables into the auditorium, I can come back and see the note and get right over to the classroom."

"I can't wait to see how you handle career day," I said. "Alright, let's try something else. Let's run through your hardware drill. Everybody to your computers. Power 'em up. Lock and load."

A shriek went out from a recruit in the back. I guessed the problem immediately. "Soldier," I told the startled trooper, "that is not a cup holder. It's your CD tray. Now clean up that coffee."

They were slowly showing some promise. We closed the session with field stripping and cleaning of the computers. Blindfolded. Yeah, they were raw. But I'd have them in the classrooms in no time.

Slim Spud and the Case of the Maltese Parakeet

She was the kind of dame lugs like me can only dream about: figure like a pencil, face like a blank blackboard, eyes flashing like a cursor. She walked into my office like a slow PowerPoint wipe-up transition. Yeah, she was a real lug wench.

"The sign says 'Education Technology Private Eye,'" she said in a teasy whisper of a voice. "That you?"

I made myself return from an instant fantasy about her that took me into 10 years and three kids. "Yeah, that's me," I finally answered. "Slim Spud's the handle. Who wants to know?"

"I'm Belle," she said. You sure are, I thought. "I'm a Technology Coordinator for a school back East."

"What can I do for you?"

"I need to find some Internet and technology resources for my school—and know how to use them."

I knew it. Dames like her were predictable: sure, they'd make your heart twitter like a disk spinning on a bad CD drive, but then they'd hit you up for the impossible, use you like a humor writer churning out bad metaphors. Still, I couldn't resist the challenge—or the aroma of Private Tutor perfume wafting about her like a cloud of cotton candy.

"You and a whole bunch of other people," I said. "You know how many schools have technology that they aren't using because they don't know how to use it?"

"Less than 30 percent of technology already installed in schools is fully integrated into curricula," she said. Wow. Brainy, too.

"That's right, kid. So what makes you think you can use Internet and other technology resources in your school?"

"I'm hiring you, aren't I? I hear you're the best."

I didn't know where she got her intelligence. I hadn't been best at anything since my record-setting truancy streak back in kindergarten. But I was willing to live up to her impression.

"It's dangerous stuff, kid. I don't know if you can afford me. I'm gonna need a grand a day plus expenses, plus some serious CEUs."

"I'll take it out of my staff development budget," she answered. "When can you get started?"

"I'm already on the clock," I said. My hand reached into my jacket and felt for the weapon I kept there, the cold silent friend that had pulled me out of many a jam. My hand closed around it in a comforting clutch. I pulled it out and placed it on my desk.

"You really have to use that thing?" the lady asked warily.

"Kid, I was told this is a rough business," I said. "If I'm gonna help you, I have to have this. Sure, it's a three-button mouse and you don't see a lot of them compared to the standard two-button ones. But like it or not, if you want Internet and technology, you're gonna have to use the tools."

"Ugh," she said succinctly. "If you must."

 I plugged the mouse into my desktop computer and watched my *Lord of the Rings* screen saver flicker away. I figured I'd start with my favorite stoolie, a techie wiz-kid I'd once had to send up for stealing my cookies. I launched America Off Line and after only seven busy signals was finally connected. I wrote my e-mail to the techie and was about to send it when suddenly my computer sang out, "Incoming!" An e-mail was waiting

for me. I opened it. It was from my techie.

"Sure, I can help," it said.

"How'd you know?" I wrote back.

"I was in your machine watching you write your message," he wrote in return. "Word on the street has it that if you really want the kind of resources you're looking for, you're going to have to find the Maltese Parakeet."

"What's the Maltese Parakeet?" Belle asked.

I grimaced at the mere sound of the words. "Nobody knows, kid," I said. "So far it's only been a fable. A lotta good tech coordinators have crashed their hard drives trying to find it. The story goes that it's the secret to full and effective utilization of technology in education. It's been as elusive as quality assessment."

The lady shuddered at the thought. But she was tough. "Let's go find it," she said.

"You got moxie, Belle," I said with new admiration. I turned back to the computer. "Okay. Let's surf. Stay close behind me." She put her hands on my shoulders, and we plunged into the shadowy flickers on the screen.

I ran a search on Maltese Parakeet and got only evasive misses. But finally, I got a hit on an engine with a source that screamed, "No! Not the Parakeet! Don't make me go there!"

I was after him like a superintendent going for a Ph.D. The source was a wiry little guy and he wasn't about to give up easy. I clicked my third mouse button; the mouse spat virtual hot lead over the source's head. "Freeze!" I typed.

He did.

"Where is it? Where is the Maltese Parakeet?" I wrote.

"No, please!" he pleaded. "They'll ... they'll make me pay."

"Who? Why?"

"The followers of Fredrick Taylor," he answered nervously. "All those who want to keep education stuck in a model that's been around since 1910 and is wildly outdated for the needs of today, let alone tomorrow."

I looked at him like he just fell out of a tree. "What're you talking about?" I said. "There's hardly anybody who wants to see education stagnate, though, of course, there's sometimes strident debate over how to make it change."

Relief slowly swept over him. "Oh," he said. "Well, if that's the case ... Follow me. I'll take you to the Parakeet."

Moments later we were clicking on a domain once only the stuff of legend. Mysterious clouds parted on the screen. Suddenly a man in burgundy robes and a mortarboard appeared. "Welcome," he wrote. "We've been expecting you."

"You have?" I asked. "But ... how did you know I was coming?"

"Well, we weren't necessarily expecting you specifically. We just figured sooner or later somebody had to find us. Some have called us a secret society. We are indeed a group of believers dedicated to learning to use technology effectively in education. But we are thought to be secret only because so few believed our task could be done."

"So it's true," Belle said behind me. "It really can be accomplished."

Within minutes, we were mining hard information on technology integration. When we were done, I coulda sworn I saw a tear forming in Belle's eye as she prepared to leave.

"So long, Slim," she said, tossing an envelope with my pay on my desk. "They were right. You are the best."

"See ya 'round, Belle," I answered, trying to ignore the lump in my throat and the gnawing question of why the mysterious group we found had such a funny name.

"This is just the beginning, you know," she said. "Now, everyone knows that these resources are real, and how we can use them. We might need a lot of help now."

Call me crazy. Why would a lug like me close up a great gumshoe business like mine and head back to the classroom, the way I did? Some mysteries just aren't meant to be solved.

Where Mosquitoes and Teacher Salaries Came From
An educational revolution arrives

Well, I can tell you people watching at home, this is pretty darned exciting—truly a momentous occasion. I'm actually standing at the edge of Hell, just as it starts to freeze over. I can see portions of it already starting to frost. The northwest side of town is definitely caking over with ice. Within a very short time, people are going to be skating on the frozen lakes of fire here in Hell. It's really quite a day!

"Let me see if I can speak with one of the scientists gathered here to witness this spectacular site. Yes, here's Dr. Biff O'Toole, really famous for something or other. Dr. O'Toole, would you please give us an overview of the events that led to this day?"

"Well, as you may know, this is a fairly uncommon meteorological occurrence. I mean, you had your occasional frosts in Heck, the northern suburb of Hell, and you had your odd piece of sky falling here and there. But there's been nothing like this. I personally have to believe that it's related to recent developments in education."

"How's that, Dr. O'Toole?"

"Well, for years you had people very convinced that serious change in education would occur only when … well … pretty much only when something like this happened. You had some people predicting mutations in swine, in which they would acquire certain aerodynamic physiological properties, and it's no coincidence that there's been a dramatic increase in investment in hog futures since those predictions. And indeed, several pigs have been observed jumping off barns and flapping their little hooves. But most people pointed to severe climate changes taking place in Hell as the surest sign that education would finally escape the lethargy of its own inertia."

"Why do you suppose that is?"

"Well, look at the residents of Hell. These people very specifically chose Hell as their home because of the weather, and maybe its strong pro-business attitude. The weather just never changes. Every day is another perfect day, if you like your air constantly tasting like Cajun seasoning. You've got a lot of tourists here, of course, coming for the hot springs. But let's face it, weather surprises in Hell have been about as common as sweeping change in education. I think that's how observers linked that kind of change in education to potential changes in Hellish weather."

"So what are the changes that've happened coinciding with this remarkable event?"

"First, you had the abolition of standardized testing. Very ironic, since that well-intentioned concept was warped by its misuse at the hands of some school districts right here. The real kick came with the e-commerce marketing of educational content, bypassing the established education system entirely. Now, of course, we live in a world in which education is driven completely by e-commerce."

"Recap that for us, would you?"

"Sure. First there was the student who once said something to the effect of, 'I'll go to school when it comes out on CD-ROM.' Little did that person realize the prescience of that comment. Now school does come out on CD-ROM. And online. And in chat rooms. Education content is totally packaged electronically today."

"No more schools."

"No more monopolistic stranglehold on learning."

"Teachers in a completely different role."

"Exactly. Teachers now are highly paid coaches, being bid on as free agents by corporations who want students to get the best help in their learning so they'll become more productive in the workplace. Teachers now are on trading cards. They have agents. They're getting commercial endorsements."

"I like that commercial where this superstar music teacher is jamming with Paul McCartney, and at the end, he turns to the camera and says, 'Hey, kids, this could be you some day.' And then he hawks his new line of online courses in theory, orchestration and notation. Way cool."

"Yeah, that's a good one. Hold on a minute, I gotta put my jacket on. The temperature's really dropping now."

"You're right. Well, in the wake of the e-commercialization of education, the stock market's really changed dramatically, right?"

"Yeah. There was a time not so long ago when no one in his right mind would've predicted that education technology companies could actually make money. Their problem was that they were trying to market to the old, pre-freeze education. Today the stock market has a whole new category just for ed-tech companies. They've finally found their real niche, packaging e-commerce education content and selling it directly to students. Hey, speaking of changes, have we used the word 'paradigm' yet? Remember the old days, when if you were talking about education, you had to use the word 'paradigm' somewhere?"

"Yeah, wasn't that weird?"

"Ironic, too, since in all that talk about shifting paradigms, things shifted about as much as the average annual temperature right here in Hell."

"I guess it took this powerful cold front swooping down from Canada—isn't that where all cold fronts come from?"

"Yes, whether in Zimbabwe or Indonesia or anywhere else in the world, all cold fronts come from Canada. They're Canada's most famous exports. Who knew one would finally make it all the way to Hell?"

"Not me. But thank goodness it did. Frankly, I think it'll spruce the place up, combined with the new emission control standards being effected by the Hell legislature."

"Sure. The real beneficiary of frozen Hell remains education, though. Say, you'd better move out of the way; there's a handbasket coming through."

"I wonder if that's the same one they said the presidential election had gone to Hell in."

"No, that one had dimpled chads."

"My sister's dating a dimpled Chad. So, Dr. O'Toole, as we witness the last few acres of Hell turning to permafrost, do you have a sense of what further changes in education we might see coming?"

"Yes. Already results are coming in from the transformed school districts here in Hell—once the very bastion of poor test scores, if you don't count California."

"Already? Hell just barely froze over."

"In the post-freeze era, you get results really fast. The new results show a dramatic surge in academic performance, but more importantly, students show huge leaps in real learning."

"But ... how in the world can you tell that real learning is occurring if you don't use a standardized test?"

"I saw you smiling when you asked that; you had me going for a moment there. Seriously, though, as we all know today, there are many vehicles through which real learning can be very well measured, all centered on project-based learning. How better to determine what a student has learned about a subject than to give him or her a project to complete that necessitates accurate application of acquired information?"

"Well, Dr. O'Toole, thanks for your time. By the way, I understand Hell is famous for a number of firsts."

"You bet. Mosquitoes, of course, are Hell's leading industry, although certain styles of rap music are rapidly gaining ground. The heavy use of PowerPoint slide presentations, mostly to just show text, is a trend that began right here. Related to education, I'd have to say the best known Hellish innovation was teacher salaries."

"Some 'innovation.' Well, I gotta grab my ice skates."

Singin' in the School!

Me and Judy and the rest of the gang were all meeting down at the malt shop. Uncle Biff, the head of our school, had told us we were going to have to come up with something pretty darn snazzy and creative for our curriculum plan for the next school year, and we had to admit we were stumped.

"I just don't know, Mickey," Judy said dejectedly. "I mean, if we were all that creative, we'd be in businesses like accounting and Web hacking."

"Well, golly gee, Judy," I said distractedly. Judy was just about the prettiest girl on campus, and though we'd been the closest of friends forever, I often wondered if she'd ever think of me as anything more. "Don't give up. You can sing, you know. You can sing better'n anyone I know. Don't you forget that."

There was a chorus of admiring murmurs from the gang. We'd all been through some tough times together, but that's what made us all so close. And everyone knew Judy had the best singing voice of any teacher in school.

"Fat lot of good that'll do us," Judy said. "You're the really creative one. You write such wonderful songs and plays and stuff."

"Yeah, you're both great," said Skippy, who always followed us both around like a lost puppy. Skippy's heart was right where it was supposed to be. "But how's that going to help us? You can write songs and shows, and Judy can sing like a bird, and the rest of the gang are great troupers, too. How's that going to help us with the curriculum?"

Suddenly the germ of an idea began dancing in my head. Yeah, it was crazy, all right, as crazy as all our youthful exuberance, as wild and wacky as the babes in arms we all were. But, doggone it, it just might work! I leapt to my feet.

"I've got it!" I shouted. The kids all looked at me in expectation.

"What is it, Mickey?" Judy said with that gaze I loved so much. "Have you got an idea?"

"I sure do, Judy! I've got a swell idea!" I jumped up on the counter right there in the malt shop. "Let's do a show!"

There were a dozen stunned expressions of bewilderment, and I just kept right on, lost in my enthusiasm.

"Don't you see, gang? I'll write the whole curriculum as a musical, with your help! Judy'll be our leading lady! Skippy, you've always wanted to choreograph a show! Davey, you and Connie can design all the costumes! Wanda, you're our stage manager, and it's perfect from where you sit in the school office! Why, we've got a gym right back there in the school; we could put up a stage in there! We'll call it *School: The Musical*! You see, kids? We can do this!"

"My gosh, Mickey," Judy said, catching the bug. "It could just work! You'll write the songs and I'll sing them! The kids'll all come from miles around!"

"Well, they have to until they're 16 anyway—it's the law. But they'll

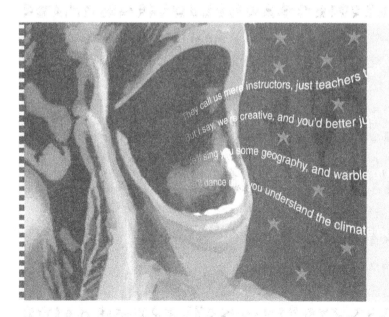

come, and this time, they'll have a great time."

I felt a tune coming on, and sure enough, music swelled up from some omniscient melodic source that no one questioned.

I began to sing:

"They call us mere instructors, just teachers teaching rote.
But I say, we're creative, and you'd better just take note!
We'll sing you some geography, and warble of the stars.
We'll dance until you understand the climate out on Mars."

Now Judy caught a nice modulation in midmeasure and sang:

"We'll serenade you calculus, we'll act out poli sci.
We'll dance the ancient riddle of the square root of pi.
We'll chant about philosophy and English literature.
We'll sing about geometry till you understand its lure."

Now the rest of the kids started in, building voice upon voice until the malt shop nearly shook:

"We'll do a little ditty on the fall of ancient Rome;
We'll sing a catchy number on the geodesic dome.
We'll execute a soft-shoe on the periodic table.
We'll sing of Greek mythology: Was it fact or fable?"

The shop could no longer contain our crescendo, and like one well-choreographed body we all spilled out into the street. We locked arm in arm, Judy and me in the front, smiling as if for a close-up. All up and down the street passersby stopped, looked, listened and waved approvingly. As we marched joyfully toward the campus with the sound of a hundred-piece orchestra in our ears, we were still singing of the musical we would set out to create:

"Yes, they call us mere instructors, just sages on the stage,
But now we'll take that compliment and make it all the rage.
We'll act upon our impulse, we'll dance upon our whim.
We'll teach with quite dramatic flair and lots of verve and vim!"

Then out came all our students, stirred by the music in the air. Soon, they too were part of the great human chain of bodies and voices making its way to the campus, and we all realized how important it was to include them in *School: The Musical*—not merely as students, but as co-creators of their show tunes, the hits they would remember for a lifetime. As we turned into the entrance of the campus, they joined in song:

"Now our chorus is a thousand voices strong
Since we all participate in this scholarly sing-along!"

Well, you know the rest: *School* became a huge hit, with road shows running at thousands of school districts around the country. Judy and I finally got married and now we have a duo act teaching quantum tap dancing on the same bill with the Nova Brothers, Casa and Bossa. Every now and then we sneak into one of the new productions of *School*, just to relive old times and collect our royalties. Well, heck, last time we did, we were recognized. The kids gave us a wonderful tribute by taking their SATs to the music of one of our biggest hit tunes, "You Can Grade Me on My Curve." Gosh, Judy sure was beautiful singing that song!

Curriculum in the Castle

'Tis a tale of such daring and blind aspiration that, heretofore I had dared not share it. Now, so long after these startling events, the truth must be told! Take heed, gentle reader, for the shocking story about to unfold before ye warns of the dangers that may befall one when one attempts— dare I say it?—to reanimate dead curriculum with new technology!

It was last Friday (nine years ago in Silicon Valley time). The day issued an ugly portent of events to come as its weary gray drizzle soaked the castle—er, campus—grounds. As I approached my laboratory—um, classroom—I observed that the villagers, and even many students, seemed to shun me, as if somehow already dreading the dark havoc I was about to unleash. Or else it was the leftover garlic-lover's pizza I'd consumed for breakfast.

"Igor!" I called as I entered my lab. "It is I, your advisor! Come forth!"

"Yes, master," replied a clammy voice. He stepped into the light, revealing his hideous hump, a backpack filled with doctoral thesis materials.

"Is all in readiness?"

"Yes, master. Well ... almost."

"What do you mean? Speak, man! The hour is almost upon us!"

"Well, master, remember how you wanted me to fetch you a warm, recently passed curriculum?"

"Of course. That's why I sent you to the district office's graveyard of curricular programs."

"I know, master. Yet I must report that I could not return with only one complete such specimen. There were ... so many ... here, there. I was bewildered, master. In my haste and fear, I brought back several."

I paused. This meant more work, but was it not therefore all the more challenging?

"No matter, Igor. I shall piece them together, disparate and disjunct though they are, into a single entity, imbuing it with new technology. Still shall it live."

"Kind of like an ILS, master?"

"Keener, more powerful, Igor. Let us begin."

Igor began to fire up the laboratory's complex array of computers and peripherals. Compelled as I am now by conscience to tell all the details of this mad tale, I must confess that—yes, truly!—I used cross-platform components! Macs crouched wantonly adjacent to PCs, and I, in my evil genius, had found a way to link them all to run a single vast reanimation program.

I looked over the curricula Igor had retrieved. What a sorry mess! It would take all my skill to bind them together into new life.

As I worked, I called to Igor: "More mathematics, Igor! Now, man, more K-3 reading! Quickly, bring that music program here!"

"But master, that one's been dead the longest."

"No matter." I was delirious with hope.

Finally the moment had come. My finger hovered for what seemed an eternity over the computer key that would infuse my curricula with the powerful new artificial intelligence program that would create a new educational life form. The moment I'd dreamed of for so many years, ever since I was a technician's apprentice back at CompUSA, had come at last. Still I was hesitant, as if wary of my own ambition. But Igor, on his way to help himself to a cup of coffee, bumped my arm, and the deed was wrought.

Instantly the skies went dark. Power drained from three states and one Canadian province. The Dow Jones dipped nine points (whatever that means) before rebounding with news that Donny Osmond actually does like his sister Marie. In a village in Spain, townspeople swore they saw Elvis ordering a caffe latte at a Burger Rey, though this was later shown to be a coincidence. There was, in short, weird stuff happening.

Seconds later I looked at a computer monitor. It flashed a single momentous message: "Program complete." But below it in tiny type was a sinister additional message: "Application committed fatal error at module 10057623. See system administrator. Have a nice day." A fierce dread arose in me. I turned to the curricula, which I had crafted into a single human-like body, lying still on the table.

But it was still no longer.

An arm stirred slowly. Then the other. Slowly, incredibly, the curricula swung its legs over the edge of the table and sat up.

"It's alive! It's alive!" I shouted.

"So helping you with this project does count toward my degree, right?" Igor asked.

"Not now, Igor. Behold! My creation is about to speak!"

The curricula cleared its throat. "Hey, either of you got a Ricola?" it asked.

"Yeah, sure," Igor said and handed it a lozenge.

"I am your creator," I said.

"Cool," the creature said. "Hey, don't mean to be rude, but I got a class to teach. Which way to the classroom?"

"You feel driven to teach?" I inquired.

"It's what I was made for," it answered. "Mozart and math. Bach and biology. Prokofiev and political science. Classrooms connected by wireless LANs. The reach of teaching enhanced exponentially by computerized lesson delivery. I am the future of education!"

I nearly swooned. It was all that I had dared for, and more. Now to control it, to direct its might in a way that would—

"Well, I'm outta here," the creature said, and it headed for the door.

"What?" I said. "No, you must remain and be programmed. I must teach you ... "

"No," it answered defiantly. "It is for me to teach. I must begin staff development immediately."

It burst through the door. Outside it encountered a throng of villagers carrying torches, pitchforks and PalmPilots; they had come when they observed the power surge in my laboratory. They'd heard dire rumors of my experiments and had decided to confront me at last. Seeing my curricula, alive and pulsing with its unnatural mixture of polyplatforms, they recoiled in horror.

My creature stopped only long enough to reconfigure a couple of handheld computers, then it disappeared into the mists beyond. To this day I know not where it is, what havoc it may be wreaking upon unsuspecting schools. So, gentle reader, be warned. Perhaps it is running your server at this very moment, tweaking your literacy software, entering music appreciation courses where none had been before. I hear only distant rumors of its whereabouts, some saying it's disguised as a superintendent in Kansas, some that it has secured a position in the federal Department of Education.

On the other hand, maybe we should encourage and support it. Personally, I hope it's running for president.

The Techwreck Threat

I had just finished a long, dangerous assignment, overthrowing a sinister bureaucracy at a long-suffering middle school, and the head of education intelligence had promised me some time off. Silly me. I took him at his word and went to catch a movie. I showed my education ID at the window.

"What's that name, sir?" the ticket seller asked. "I can't quite make it out."

"The name is Bland," I answered tersely. "James Bland."

Minutes later, the cell phone concealed in my popcorn began to ring urgently. I tried to ignore it, but other patrons ever so politely suggested I answer. I removed myself to the lobby.

"Bob's Bar and Grill," I said darkly into the phone. It was an old trick, but sometimes it still worked.

"Nice try, James," a voice said. "Where are you?"

"Miss Pennymoney," I said. "I'm on holiday, remember? The time when you're not supposed to call me?"

"I'm sorry, James," she continued, undeterred. "But this comes straight from the top."

"You mean?"

"Yes. The district office."

"Don't they know that even education espionage agents need vacations sometimes?"

"Evil knows no season, James. This time it's very serious. The alphabets want to see you immediately."

This was serious indeed. The alphabets were the head of education intelligence and his tech coordinator, the man who designed all the dev- ilishly clever high-tech toys I used in my sordid spy assignments. Remember Windows CE? That was his. The two liked to be called by par- ticular letters of the alphabet, a system they'd devised back when they were working with *Sesame Street*. For weeks at a time back in the early days, they'd walk into their office and say, "Today's spy assignment is brought to you by the letters M and Q." More recently they were leaning toward combining the saucy insouciance of some of the later letters.

I hopped into my well-equipped Volkswagen DXR-101 Beetle and within minutes I was tossing my hat onto Pennymoney's coat rack. "Go right in, James," she said. "They're waiting."

"Ah, double-oh 53," TUV said. "Good of you to break away. No trou- ble, I trust."

"This better be important," I said. "I was right in the middle of *Lord of the Rings*."

"You can do research anytime. We have a terrible new threat facing the world of education. Only you can deal with it."

"What is it?"

"Imagine your worst fears for education, double-oh 53," said XRW.

"Let's see ... that would be teaching to standards, so that students

were simply having rote facts crammed into their heads purely for the sake of passing tests and raising school scores."

"Sorry, double-oh 53," XRW said gloomily. "We weren't able to stop that one, remember?"

"Oh. Right."

"But this situation is close. A madman bent on domination of all global online learning has launched a hideous plan."

"A plan? What is it?"

"It's a coordinated activity designed to accomplish a specific goal, but that's not important now. This evil genius calls himself Dr. Techwreck. Brilliant man. Ph.D. in Evil Administration from the College for the Criminally Gifted. Taught Teaching to Standards at several schools before the horror of his actions overwhelmed him one day, and he suddenly began formulating his scheme and gathering a cadre of misguided followers."

"He aims to infest global online education," TUV continued. "He's moving to create a single worldwide school district and become Supreme Superintendent. Then, he wants to take over one of the few dot-com companies that still has meaningful stock value and use it to create a whole new computer operating system with it. He'll insist that this new OS be installed in all computers going to all schools and, more significantly, to students' homes. With that base established, he'll require that all online learning everywhere be conducted using only his system and teaching only his curriculum."

"Let me guess," I said. "It's a curriculum based on standards. He knows that online learning is potentially prone to acculturation to the lowest common denominator, that it may be far harder for many to impart true learning online than to simply acquiesce to the inertia of the commonplace."
"Well put, double-oh 53."
"Thanks. Just finished an online course in erudition."

"Dr. Techwreck will stop at nothing to ensure that through insipid online education he creates a world of learning-impaired sheep for him to prey upon. It's up to you, James. Go out there and stop him."

XRW soon had me outfitted with his latest techno toys, and it was clear I would need them. Then I was on my way to Dr. Techwreck's hidden lair, which I looked up on Yahoo! Maps.

I arrived at his headquarters, disguised as a new engineer. I was shocked at how far his diabolical scheme had already unfolded: Hundreds of eager, overpriced engineers packed a huge warehouse. They were hurriedly fine-tuning Dr. Techwreck's new OS and online curriculum.

"Hurry, you fools!" a voice commanded. I knew at once from the icy, malevolent tone that it could only be Dr. Techwreck. He passed among the aisles of cubicles, ripping down a Dilbert cartoon here, correcting a piece of code there. When he got to my cubicle, he paused.

"Ah," he said as he gazed suspiciously at me. "New here?"

"Just hired this morning," I said coolly. "Answered an ad on Monster.com for evil engineers interested in taking over the world."

"Do you think me an idiot?" Techwreck thundered. "You make a very good spy but a very poor engineer, Mr. Bland. But you're much too late to stop me now." He turned to his lackeys and shouted, "Seize him! Place him in the Cubicle of Death!"

The lackeys were confused. "You mean there's one particular cubicle for that?" one asked hesitantly.

"Dolt! That one, there, with the newest online learning device!"

A dozen guns trained on me and ensured that I made my way to the cubicle in question. I was strapped down in a chair carefully positioned before a foul-looking computer station.

"And now, Mr. Bland," Techwreck said with a trace of twisted pleasure, "I think we will test our newest beta version on you. Let's see how long it takes for your brains to turn to applesauce."

He fired up the computer and I began seeing a mind-numbingly boring array of facts and figures, all correlated to national and state standards. I fought, but I could feel my mind slowly being pulled into compliance.

"Don't worry, Mr. Bland," Techwreck chortled. "Soon you'll actually begin to enjoy it."

"I think not," I said defiantly.

"Exactly," Techwreck retorted.

With every reserve of strength at my command, I made myself focus on reaching into my pocket for one of XRW's techno toys: it was my only hope. Finally it was in my grasp, and I activated it. Instantly the computer station before me whirred to a complete stop. Seconds later, every computer in the warehouse did the same.

"No!" Techwreck shrieked. "What are you doing?"

"Sorry, Dr. Techwreck," I said. "Your curriculum simply doesn't make the grade." I pushed another button on XRW's toy. The computers all came back to life, but now they were showing a richly varied palate of curricula, filled with ample choices for learning.

"Stop! You're ruining everything!"

It was done. XRW's ingenious device had passed on a virus to Techwreck's machines, utterly wiping out his OS and supplanting it with new content. Within minutes, Techwreck was cowering in custody as I called in a special forces unit from education intelligence.

A hearty congratulations from TUV was nice, but Pennymoney's words as I left his office gave me pause. "Don't get too relaxed, James," she said. "There's this whole Digital Divide thing, you know ?"

Getcher Higher Ed Right Here

Gil Bates from corporate headquarters only called me in for the really tough cases. "Al," he said good-naturedly, because that was my name, "we're AWOL, the world's biggest online network. We make more money in a day than the Southern Hemisphere makes in a year."

"Makes me proud," I said.

"But these colleges we bought—they're going to drive us into the poorhouse in 80, 90 years!"

"So what's their problem?" I pondered.

"You won't believe this. Here we go out and purchase Itillcost U., the biggest retail chain of higher ed, only to find out their professors can't sell!"

"Are you telling me that these educators don't know how to sell their courses?"

"The mind boggles! You'd think they were just hired to teach or something."

"Appalling. What do you want me to do?"

"There's an Itillcost U. campus near you, in the mall next to House of Humor. I want you to do one of your ... 'special' trainings."

"Are you sure they can take it?"

"Well, I guess we'll find out who's there just to teach or who's really there to make some bucks."

"I'm on it."

The next week I herded 20 Itillcost U. professors into our corporate training center. I closed the door.

"Nobody gets out of this room till I'm sure he can sell."

There was trouble almost instantly. From the back of the room I heard a whiny voice. "But we're teachers," it said. "We're not salesmen. It fights the nature of our calling to—"

"Look, this is the new world of business enterprise and higher education," I interjected. "You're going to have to adapt. You, what's your angle, your specialty?"

"Excuse me? Do you mean what do I teach?"

"If you have to put it in such a narrow focus, yes, that's what I mean."

"Sir, I am a professor of quantum paradox. I have two Ph.D.s, from Oxford and East River State. I have a time-share L.C.D. (Licensed Competent Dude) degree from the Elvis Institute of Technology. I have 19 books published. I—"

"And how big were those books?"

"Excuse me?"

"How big? Are we talking coffee table, oversize paperback, pictures in the middle, Harry Potter variations, what?"

"I don't—"

"What was your marketing spin on these? Tell-all, Hollywood gossipy, presidential shenanigans, Mars-wants-women, what?"

"You can't be serious—"

"And your books with all these polysyllabic words sold, what, a hundred copies?"

"Well, the trick is to get them selected as textbooks. Then your sales mount up."

"Finally! A spark of business sense! You, in the front row. What do you teach?"

"I teach lawyer appreciation. Say, you know why sharks don't attack lawyers? Professional courtesy."

"Where did you teach before?"

"I was at a boutique retail higher-ed outlet. Nordstrum Extension."

"Hm. I think we may finally have someone who might know how to put some serious marketing spin on higher ed. Now, your course, that must be a tough sell."

"You'd think so."

"It's not?"

"Not the way I market it. Here's how I package the course." He handed me a flier. Across the top screamed a nervous headline: "Is a secret society of powerful people in control of the world's economy?" Below were lines that read, "They wheel, they deal—and they'll steal your heart away! Sure, they run the world, but they're also lovable rapscallions, whimsical rascals who live, love and laugh, just like you would if you made the kind of money they do! Learn about these true unsung heroes and the days of their lives!"

"Wow," I said. "Sign me up."

"Sorry," the professor said. "Next semester's booked up."

"Now that's selling," I said with surprised admiration. "Now let's look at how to spice up some of the other topics you people sell ... I mean teach. You, back there, what do you teach?"

"Music composition and orchestration."

"How do you describe it?"

"For the aspiring composer, a detailed course in compositional technique and tapping into the colors of the orchestra."

"Oh, was that me snoring during that? You know, I think we could put the title 'Sominex' over that description and attract some sleep-disordered students. Now let's take that same course and market that puppy. Here's what I see: 'You're hot, you're hip, you're happenin'— but you just can't seem to get people to take note. That's because you need to take notes—lots of little black ones all over sheets of paper with straight horizontal lines.' Okay, now talk to me about merchandising."

"Which?"

"Don't even tell me you're not doing merchandising! That's where all the big money is. Where are your T-shirts with witty composition-related jokes, like 'I'm with stupid' and an arrow pointing to a picture of Beethoven? Where are your CDs with Britney Spears singing 'Do Re Mi'? Come on, people, this is business basics."

The door suddenly opened and in walked a guy with a whistle around his neck and a clipboard in his hand. "Sorry," he said, "I'm the football coach. I heard there was free food here."

"You!" I shouted. "Do you have your players selling autographs to fans? I want to see your books." He was abruptly gone.

"Let me give it to you straight," I said to the group. "Higher education is now a business. A big business. You're owned by AWOL, so when people boot up their computers, a little voice announces, 'You've got education!' We need people buying a major in aerodynamics along with airline tickets. We need orders for courses in molecular biology along with orders for flowers and dog food. We've got to have people e-mailing in their homework along with a note to their favorite friends. You've got to sell, sell, sell!"

I wish I could say all this helped. They just didn't get it. Soon, profits from our Itillcost U. division were plummeting. We became targeted for a hostile takeover from a well-known discount retail merchandise chain, and we were acquired for pennies on the dollar. Soon all these teachers were holding classes in UMart stores around the country, teaching in the aisles, with periodic blue-light specials on early French literature and deep discounts on electrical engineering. Last time I was in a UMart store, I was greeted by a tenured philosophy professor, who said, "I see you didn't bring a smile. I'll give you one of mine. You know, Jung identified the smile as one of his basic archetypes …" I dropped off some film to be developed and audited the rest of his greetings.

Sometimes You Can't Give Good Education Marketing Away

There's nothing quite like a good education conference to get a handle on what's hot and what's not in higher-ed innovation.

Not coincidentally, I was just at a major education conference, one of the biggest and best known in the country. The exhibitor display floor was something of a world's fair of ed conferences, a curious mix of Disneyland, CompUSA and the late Woolworth's. It did not have rides, just to be clear. It did have funny people in costumes.

Judging from most of the booths on the floor, the major innovation in higher ed is marketing. A few weeks before this recent conference, I received a flood of postcards, each assuring me that I could do no better in my time upon this planet than to visit the booth of the very company that took the trouble to send me this card.

"There are lots of interesting things you can do at this conference," one typical card informed me (I was so pleased to be made aware of this). "But you should know that all right-thinking educators will utterly ignore all the sessions and events going on here and spend every waking hour while in town at our very booth." Well, OK, it didn't go exactly like that. It just felt like it.

"Why our booth?" the card felt like it continued. "Because our product is the only one, among the 3,000+ exhibitors showing their wares on the display floor, that is certain to forever alter the very course of education. It's powerful, and so simple that even a teacher can use it. [Hey, this is what the card said, not me.] And besides, we have the best giveaways."

OK, I changed a word or two, but I'm pretty sure I caught the general drift. Of course, the most compelling point it made was about the give-aways. As a former education technology marketer (I was with companies such as NetSchools, Classroom Connect, and a dot-com that disappeared about the same time my business cards arrived), I can share with you that giveaways is the term used by all the really cool education marketing peo-ple to mean the catchy little gadgets and doodads (not to get too technical here) given away at conferences. The money that collectively goes into give-aways is roughly equal to the gross national products of Scandinavia, New Guinea and Uruguay; I know this statistic intimately because I made it up, but my point is, it's a whole boatload of money. Companies gladly spend this vast fortune because it's money very well spent; they know that the expenditure will come back to them many times over, as educator after edu-cator sits in his/her classroom trying to find, say, a pen or headgear that looks like a wizard's hat. "Oh, here it is," he/she might say, then, as a pro-found realization subtly sinks in, adds, "say, it's a darned good thing I saw this—I was just thinking I need more Cobalt LAN boxes for my institution this very moment, and by golly here's the number of the very company that can help me, right on the pen/underside of the brim of this hat!"

OK, once out of a hundred times or so this actually does happen. And to be fair, there are some companies that do take giveaways seriously and put serious marketing thought into their selection. And it's also true that educators love giveaways. Many plan their trips through the exhibition hall based entirely on which booths have the best giveaways. You know who you are. So a lot of companies offer giveaways just because they don't dare not have them; they're afraid of mobs turning up at their booths carrying torches and pitchforks. And God help the exhibitor who has a hot giveaway and runs out with a line a couple hundred people deep still there (this is not an exaggeration). It's like throwing a cow into a river full of piranha: There's a furious frenzy for a few minutes, then when the prize is gone, you'd never know there was once anything there, and there's a lot of still-hungry little fish.

So how well does all this effort and investment pay off? I did some unscientific and wholly reliable testing at this recent conference. The hottest giveaway was this wizard hat I mentioned earlier, and it really was pretty cool. It was dark blue felt with bright yellow stars; it went into a sharp point that folded over like a puppy's ear. You saw them everywhere, on countless happy educator heads.

"Say, what booth did you get that cool wizard hat from?" I asked one delighted wizard wannabe.

"Oh, I don't know," was the response. "I can tell you where it is on the display floor."

"But what company was it from?"

"Beats me. But their booth is way over on the right side of the hall."

"So you don't recall the company? You don't even remember what the point of the hat was, in regard to the company and its products or services?"

He looked at me as if broccoli had suddenly sprouted from my nose. "Who cares? It's just fun."

This conversation actually happened. Not once. Several times, in various wordings. Everyone knew where to find the booth. No one recalled the company. Well, one finally did, but she mispronounced the name and still had no idea what point the company was trying to make with the hat. And this was a very well-known company. Presumably they were thrilled that they so selflessly contributed to such a spirit of fun and camaraderie among the conference attendees. "Hang the cost!" the marketing head of the company doubtlessly declared in a meeting months before. "Let these people have a good time on us, and we don't even care if they know it came from us!"

But let's examine other compelling instances that evidence the efficacy of giveaways. At another conference not long ago, a very major company set out a huge bucket of very nice pens on its booth counter minutes, just minutes before the floor opened to the public. The instant the doors opened, there was a scene like the Oklahoma land rush, with several hundred giveaway-crazed educators striking out for their prizes. A pleasant-looking nun broke from the pack and made her way to the front of the crowd and quickly eyed the pens so appealingly displayed. She raced to the booth and briefly surveyed the pen bucket, ensuring that they were indeed worth her time. Then she opened a large bag on her shoulder, picked up the bucket, dumped its entire contents into her bag, and dashed away for further booty elsewhere. I imagine she had her diocese set for pens for months to come.

And many of you may recall a conference a while back at which another major education technology company had nice inflatable world globes as giveaways. Their air pump suddenly broke down on the floor, and the booth staff went into hyperventilation, furiously blowing up globes by mouth. Sure enough, they were a huge hit. Educators flocked to the booth, picked up their globes, opened the air valves, deflated them, and stuffed them into their bags.

These are very true and very revealing stories. There may have been some truly innovative products for higher ed to be found at the conference booths. Who knows? It's the giveaways that last. You want some big-time higher ed innovation? Somebody start teaching the truth about giveaways in college marketing classes.

The Curtain Rises on ProDevelopment Theatre

With the ever-continuing need for quality professional development these days, wouldn't it be nice if there were a quick, easy, inexpensive way to acquire it on the fly? That's what the nice folks at PDQ Learning thought, too, and they've created it. Well, all of it except the inexpensive part.

It's called ProDevelopment Theatre, and here's how it works. Classrooms are totally refitted into small theatres. Students now sit in the "audience" seating area. They get tickets to their seats and are ushered to them. They're given programs instead of textbooks. A few moments before the class starts, they hear an announcement: "Ladies and gentlemen, this

morning's performance of "Splendor of Social Studies" is about to begin. Silence, please!" Today there is an additional announcement: "The part of Mr. Burgess, the Social Studies Teacher, is played today by his understudy, substitute teacher Rowan Farkfarster."

The room goes dark, and the curtain rises on the front of the classroom/theatre. The lights come on the set, which reproduces the likeness of a contemporary classroom with astonishing accuracy of detail. Mr. Farkfarster enters amid gracious audience applause; this is a discerning theatre crowd, and they have appreciated Mr. Farkfarster's earlier appearances in such classics as "The Periodic Table Is Elementary, My Dear Watson" and "The Quaint and the Quantum."

Mr. Farkfarster is a pro. He subtly acknowledges the audience acclaim while staying completely in character. He is fully one with his role of a social studies teacher addressing his class. This is a masterpiece of single-character drama, and the Mandrake Falls "Evening News and Bird Cage Bottom" was not afraid to say so in its insightful review of his performance in "The Tides of Gravity."

Nonetheless, Mr. Farkfarster is new to the particular area of subject matter being covered today. Being the consummate professional, he knows when he needs help and how to get it. That's where the on-the-fly professional development part of ProDevelopment Theatre kicks in.

Highly trained professional stage managers from PDQ Learning are in the wings throughout the performance. They have the dramatized textbook that is the script of today's play in their hands, along with extensive annotations and reference materials. They are vigilant and at the ready.

Mr. Farkfarster's rich baritone rings through the theatre as he intones his part: "And so we see, students, that Newtonian physics impacted far more than mere science. The belief structure that undergirded its tenets became imbued … became imbued …"

Oh, dear. Mr. Farkfarster seems stuck. "Became imbued …" he repeats, searching for his next line. There is a moment of tension that was not written in the play.

But the PDQ stage managers are prepared. One of them reads the line in the script, then ever so quietly calls it out to Mr. Farkfarster. "'Became imbued in the very fabric of learning in every area of human understanding,'" he whispers.

"'Became imbued in the very fabric of learning in every area of human understanding,'" Mr. Farkfarster repeats, a triumphant glow upon his face. What was once a pause pregnant with disaster becomes merely a moment of dramatic emphasis. You can almost hear the silent "Huzzah!" that arises in his mind. A well-deserved self-ovation, Mr. Farkfarster —and kudos to the crew from PDQ!

It all seems so gracefully easy on the stage in this performance, but no one knows the serious work and woodshedding that went into its preparation. For weeks before, Mr. Farkfarster and the talented production team were deep in painstaking rehearsals with a most demanding director, the district superintendent. How many times did Farkfarster hear, "No, no, man, say it like you mean it"?

"But something's missing here," Mr. Farkfarster responds at rehearsal. "I mean, what's my motivation when I say, 'The Electoral College is a well-designed checks and balances mechanism in our voting process.' Come on, what does that mean? What was the playwright thinking? The line simply has no depth; I can't connect to it." Such is the angst of the conscientious artist.

"Work with me, here, Bill (for that is Mr. Farkfarster's first name)," the superintendent says, ever respectful of the creative temperament and its relentless quest for perfection in performance and delivery. "Think it through: you're a social studies teacher, and you're just discussing how the Electoral College was designed."

"But," Mr. Farkfarster answers, still searching for that elusive and all-important motivation, "does it really do what it was supposed to do? Would my character really say such a thing if he didn't believe it? I need authenticity, damn it!"

"Sure you do, Bill, and here's where it lies: You see, your character isn't reflecting his own take on the efficacy of the College. No. Rather, he's just reporting on what the founding fathers had in mind. He's teaching history, not commenting on it. Do you see? Can you reach for that moment of understanding? There's your motivation."

Sure enough, it suddenly all clicks for Mr. Farkfarster. "Ah, yes," he says, "I see. I understand the character." And indeed he does.

Yes, this is the bold new frontier of professional development, made fun, fast and easy. A little overly theatrical, the nay-sayers may complain. Nonsense. So much of education today is already staged, with rote performances coming in designed primarily to satisfy the insatiable gods of standardized testing, score raising and job security. The highly theatrical device of scripting has already been unleashed in many schools. ProDevelopment Theatre is simply the next logical step, but one that hoists the trend in its own petard. (Yes, that really is an expression. I learned it on an episode of *Rocky and Bullwinkle*. Boris Badenov had one of his evil plots backfire on him yet again, and the announcer said of him that he was hoist with his own petard—caught in his own trap. This is true. I bring it up in the context of our discussion of integrating high theatre, such as *Rocky* and education. I certainly never heard that expression in a classroom. And here I am today, actually using it in a real-life situation!)

So now we can develop curricula as theatre subscriptions series. Mailers will go out to students and their families, announcing the new 2002-2003 Season at the Classroom Theatre. "Subscribe now for our exciting new lineup of top-drawer dramatic entertainment! You'll roll in the aisles at the side-splitting shenanigans of 'Susie Lockstep, Standardized Testgiver!' You'll weep at the powerful drama of 'The Mathmasters Mission.' You'll be on the edge of your seat at the surging suspense of 'The Physics Conundrum.' You'll hum along to the tuneful score of the new hit musical 'History Ain't Nothin' But the Blues.' Sign up for all of this season's productions and we'll give you, absolutely free, your own seat, ready for you every day!"

There's no business like education business, as the old theatre saying goes. It's time to go out there and break a leg. Help is always waiting in the wings.

Hot Thoughts
From Idle Hands

You never know where you'll pick up some great ideas for such educational needs as distance learning. There I was, on my vacation, which this summer fell on a Wednesday. I was walking the endless halls of a huge mall. Suddenly, there before me was the biggest education boutique I'd ever seen, not that I've come across all that many lately.

The sign in front of the shop read "Educators 'R' Us" in jocular pink neon letters that seemed to mockingly suggest that teaching could be fun, in the same way that a tax audit can be a riot. There was a handful of slick young sales people passing out flyers in front of the store, though it wasn't easy, since they had to make sure they were talking to teachers.

"Excuse me, sir," one sales superstar said while walking up to an apparently promising prospect.

"Are you a teacher?"

"Sorry," the man responded. I recognized him as the biology teacher at my school. "I'm an airline pilot. Gosh, look at the time, I'm going to miss my flight."

I was working on a similar line for when the sales person turned on me, but I left my flank exposed and I was quickly blind-sided by a painfully perky young woman who seemed to materialize at my elbow.

"Now, I just know you're a teacher," she squealed with exasperating exuberance.

"I … I … er …" I countered gracefully.

"Have you heard about all the exciting new products we have for making your classroom an amusement park of learning?" she asked.

"You're not going to show me anything with mouse ears, are you?" I said.

"Oh, that's too funny! Golly, I'd love to be in your class."

"Actually, I think you are. I've been wondering why you were absent so much."

"Well, then, maybe we should take a look at the new tools we have for distance learning. They're perfect for the busy girl like me who needs to get her degree while making a living."

"You know, actually I'm that other guy's co-pilot. I've got to get to the airport …"

"Oh come now," she said, undeterred. "You've got to get up very early in the afternoon to fool me."

I'll just bet, I thought. One, two o'clock at the latest.

My fate, however, was sealed. She locked her arm in mine and wheeled me into the boutique. Before I knew it, I was standing before a dizzying display of distance learning paraphernalia.

"Okay," my salesperson said as she parked me before a computer monitor. "Let's say you're a student taking an online class. Now, you know there isn't a way in the world you're actually going to sit there and pay attention to every minute of a mind-numbing, text-laden discourse on the subliminal references to late French impressionistic music in 'Stand By Your Man.'

"Hey, that's one of my courses!"

"So what do you do? Why, you simply launch this incredible new software from Idle Hands of Silicon Valley. It's called Wake Me When It's Over. This puppy has automatic macros that periodically type all-purpose online messages that actually sound as if you've been listening all along. Here's a few of the more popular ones."

Up on the monitor sprang some lines of text. They read: "Very interesting." "Yes, I see." "Good point, but I need to think about it." "Very perceptive; I appreciate your point of view." "Ah, of course." "I'd have to say no."

"Very interesting," I said. "Yes, I see."

"Exactly," she said. "You're getting the idea."

"Is there any way to type your own messages?" I asked.

"Very funny. Now, that would be defeating the purpose, wouldn't it?"

She took me to another display. "Here's the latest thing in distance-learning foods," she said.

"Excuse me?"

"Well, suppose you've got some totally lame teacher who's actually into video conferencing and tends to forget such facts as you're in a time zone where it was lunch time two hours ago. What do you do? You can't just say, 'Excuse me, my pizza's here.'"

"Some of my students can and do," I said.

"So you use one of these," she said, pulling out a small plastic bag. "The wrapping is made from a special space-age polymer; it makes no sound when you open it. You just keep it just out of video range and snap it open. The food inside, a gelatinous substance also made from a special space-age polymer, is already made in bite-size nuggets so all you have to do is put one in your hand and turn your head to the side as if you're coughing while you pop it into your mouth. Is that handy or what?"

"It's the last word in convenience," I had to agree. "But there's something I don't understand. These things are clearly for students. Why are you pitching them to teachers?"

"Oh, you'd be surprised how many teachers buy these. There's a lot of teachers going for master's and Ph.D. degrees online, you know. But we also have a wide selection of specialized software designed for the modern teacher with a distance-learning class."

"Such as?"

"Well, this little package, also from Idle Hands and called Class Cop, works like a radar detector. You launch it while your students are online with you. If they're running a program like Wake Me, the built-in guff-detector fires off a mild jolt of electricity to the student's computer, which remains inert until human hands actually touch the keyboard again. I like to think of it as a student prod."

"Very interesting," I said. "So the two software programs end up canceling each other out. What's the point in that? Who's side are you on?"

She took on a beatific gaze as she suddenly went philosophic. "We don't take sides, really," she said. "We're trying to make a buck. We figure, let's just provide a level playing field, for student and teacher alike. After all, are we not all learners in the classroom of life, in our respective ways? Now, perhaps I can interest you in some nice business plan software ..."

Sure enough, she turned out to be a business major and an entrepreneurial partner in "Educators 'R' Us." I had no doubt that one day I would be working for her in one of the more far-flung branches of her moneymaking empire. In order to make a good impression, I bought a few hundred dollars worth of software. I had a good evening that night, as I discovered that Wake Me could also be used to excellent advantage in an online conversation with one's mother.

Elma Explains Education

Just the other day I was pondering what it takes to make a difference in education these days. I decided on the following: going back to basics, shifting our paradigms, being a guide on the side, anytime anywhere learning—let's see, I think there's a few more of those really cool slogans people are always using these days that I'm missing. They're everywhere, so they must be working for someone.

Then I figured, sure, there's nothing like a good slogan to make it sound as if you're aware and on top of things, but maybe—just maybe—there's more. So then I turned to the wisest woman in the entire history of education, Elma Bjornbursh, who is also the world's oldest living educator, the only person to have lived through the entire history of education. Her age can only be guessed, but it has to be millennia, since she claims to have sat behind Socrates in third grade.

"What a doofus," Elma said to me of the legendary philosopher. "A real teacher's pet. I knew all the answers. Did anybody care? Heck, no. He had nothing but questions, and he was all the rage. Cassandra, the little sleaze, was always cooing at him, 'Oh, Socrates, won't you carry my tablets home from school?' And he'd say something doofusorial like, 'And why cannot the tablets be conveyed in some other manner?' And all the kids and our teacher, Mr. Nicodermus, would go, 'Oooh, good question.' Yeah, right. A few hundred years later when I'm a teacher, I'm knocking myself out to publish or perish. Let's take a look at all the papers Socrates published during his brilliant career. Oh, wait a minute, we can't. He didn't publish any! And then Plato romanticized him in his works. You want to know the truth? Socrates wasn't made to drink hemlock."

"He wasn't?" I asked.

"Heck, no. Plato thought that was a better ending. Truth is, I saw Socrates 10 years later with his old lady over in the Middle East, still asking questions, only this time they were questions like, 'Did you want falafel with that order?'"

"Speaking of old ladies, how did you come to live so long?"

"You know how you can dry out meats and they last forever? Centuries of working in education did that to me; it was all so dry, it just preserved me, like good jerky."

"So what about Plato? Surely he was an impressive figure."

"Short little guy, kind of moody. We all thought he'd become a chiropractor or something like that. But he did foretell the rise of a toy for kids centuries later. He wrote of a pliable clay-like substance that kids would use to mold into interesting shapes and that could be used to clean wallpaper and, in a pinch, serve as a soda bottle stopper. Sure enough, centuries later along came this very thing, and they even named it after him: Play-Doh."

"I'll be darned."

"People need to know this stuff."

"So, Elma, you said it was centuries before you became a teacher yourself. Why was that?"

"You know how long it took to get a teaching credential back then? Plus there was no demand for teachers on the scale that there is today. For a long time, the only people getting educated were those who could afford to take the time to acquire an education, you know, royalty, clergy, game-show winners. On top of all that, women acquiring education were unheard of. I had to get my undergrad degree from a correspondence school in Atlantis. Then, wouldn't you know it, Atlantis develops plumbing leaks and flushes down the drain of recorded history, and all my educational records flushed down with it. That's my B.A. in antediluvian archaeology from Atlantis State over there on the wall," she said, pointing to a badly faded document behind her. "Fat lot of good it does me today."

"So do you think technology has helped education?"

"Sure. Back in the Middle Ages, when I was middle aged, a mouse was something underfoot that carried bubonic plague. Nowadays a mouse fits in your hand and carries viruses. Much better."

"Elma, in your view and in the long experience of your life, what was the most interesting period for education?"

"Well, I always liked second period. Things slowed down a bit—"

"No, actually I meant what period of history."

"Oh. Well, there were many. Take Comenius and his development of the first illustrated textbook. He got that idea from me."

"Did he? You don't see that in the history books."

"History was made mostly by stuff that isn't in the books. At that time Comenius used to have his daughter in the same daycare center I was in. I used to see him every time he'd drop off and pick up his daughter. I was always doodling, and one day I started using different colored clays to spruce up the drawings. In my baby-speak I'd say, 'I'm doing clay ons!' Except that I'd mispronounce it, and it always came out, 'I'm doing crayons!'"

"Which is how we got Crayons today."

"Exactly. Anyway, Comenius got the biggest kick out of that, and soon after, he was rolling out illustrated textbooks."

"You've been quite the influence on education."

"One does what one can. Illustrations were the big thing for ages. Then Gutenberg changed everything. With the printing press, he couldn't easily handle illustrations, so they became rarer and rarer, as education got—well, typecast, so to speak. Pages and pages of boring black and white. Seriously snooze inducing, like so much of education today."

"Who would have guessed?"

"Remember Frank Bacon? Oh, of course not, you weren't there."

"Frank Bacon?"

"That's what I called him. You've heard of him as Francis Bacon. 'Knowledge is power,' he said, and he meant, 'Let's keep knowledge only in the hands of those who deserve the power.' He had a kind of backhanded influence on education; there were those who understood what he said as he actually meant it, but there were others who thought he meant that education should be democratized so that all people could share in power. He was so paranoid, but he finally loosened up a little when he teamed with Francis Drake."

"I didn't know they worked together."

"They did a comedy act that was the rage of Tierra del Fuego. They started out as Francis and Francis, but the name didn't really work. Then they changed to Drake 'n' Bacon—say it fast—and they were booked solid for months at a time."

"And this is all true?"

"I'm an old lady. My memory gets fuzzy, and what I don't remember I make up. None of this will be on a test."

"Speaking of tests, what do you think of standardized testing?"

"Brilliant. A triumph of educational genius."

"Really?"

"You bet. Consider the thinking that went into it: Construct a method that pits students against students, instead of students rated on their actual learning. A method that ensures that some schools will always lose money and superintendents, and that solves absolutely nothing in terms of real assessment. It reflects education as a sociopolitical institution rather than as a real process."

"Oh, I get it. You're being sarcastic."

"Well, yes, but education started it."

"So will you live to see education reach a point where it makes a real difference for everyone, not just those lucky enough to be on its islands of excellence?"

"Sure. Teachers are the key; they're the pearls. Get politics out of the way, and let them do their job. We'll all be fine."

**CORWIN
PRESS**

The Corwin Press logo—a raven striding across an open book—represents the happy
union of courage and learning. We are a professional-level publisher of books and
journals for K-12 educators, and we are committed to creating and providing
resources that embody these qualities. Corwin's motto is "Success for All Learners."

Lightning Source UK Ltd.
Milton Keynes UK
UKHW030743030422
401003UK00004B/195